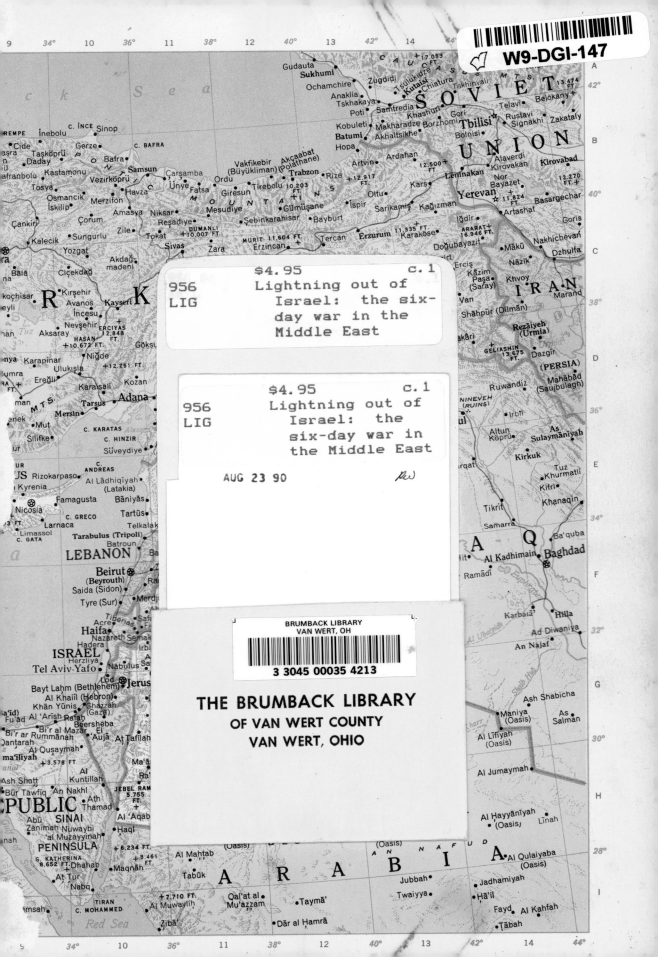

LIGHTNING OUT OF ISRAEL

THE SIX-DAY WAR IN THE MIDDLE EAST

THE ASSOCIATED PRESS

FOREWORD

Associated Press correspondents have covered every war since the American Civil War. Some have died on the battlefields. But no war has brought the pressures of time and shifting focus as did the three-front, six-day blitz by Israel's air and ground forces which staggered and defeated the forces of four Arab nations.

The swift victory stunned the rest of the world. How it was won, the day-by-day chronicle of the men who fought it and the citizens who endured it, the glory and the tragedy of it, are the subjects of this book. The material was gathered by Associated Press newsmen, some of them working in the hostility of war-torn nations.

It is to these devoted Associated Press newsmen in the Middle East, London, New York and other contributing bureaus that this volume is dedicated.

Wes Gallagher
General Manager
The Associated Press

CONTENTS

PROLOGUE

The Promised Land. Promised to whom?

The Jew, who came first? Or the Arab, who was there last?

These cousins of the Semitic peoples would say, the both, that the land is the pledge of their God. But which God: Jehovah or Allah? What God hath joined together, let no man put asunder. But man had, this to the Jew, that to the Arab.

Would that these Children of their Gods could live in their House, as one, in peace. But the House was too haunted, and the Children had too much the knowledge of their ages.

In the early sun the child of Gideon could look down from his streaking jet on Sinai where his Moses had sealed a covenant with God. And the Arab could look, too, look into the blue eyes of his son and see in them the trace of the ancient Phoenician who bought and sold in commerce when those who had divided his land wore the skins of the animal. This ancient had been the bearer of man's most precious gift, the number and the letter. And this gift had been turned on his child in the words that said part of the land of his ancestor was not to be his.

But the avenger in his jet could say equally that justice rode with him. Three times his people had been ripped from their home and strewn until all that remained of their Caanan was a book and a law and a God. Was a man to be judged because he could still smell the burning sandalwood of his Temple, hear the hoof drum of the Cossack who brought pogrom on the arc of his blade, feel the weight of his people falling upon him one after another from the lip of the pit at Belsen as the machine pistol bucked in the

hand of the German? Let him who is without sin cast the first stone. But what of him who is sinned against? As his leathered fingers tightened on the bomb release of his plane could he be judged for saying "So be it" considering all that had been?

Wasn't this man David loosing his stone against the glowering brow of Goliath? Surely the image appeals.

But who could see Goliath in the ragged Arab refugee who for 19 years had hungered and watched across a line made by others at someone else tilling the land Allah had willed him?

So much had been born of this land. Three faiths that worshipped a God each said was The One. Three cultures and one of them would not be great until the Crusaders came to seize their Godhead and stayed to learn from those who lived in this crossroads of the world.

The fate of this land had been sealed at Creation. It had been made a keystone in the arch of three continents carrying the weight of caravans and kings who passed its way. The people had prospered from their caravans and fought with their kings. Always. If this was the Fertile Crescent, so was it bloody.

So it would be in June, 1967, because Allah had willed and Jehovah had covenanted and man had taken and other men would redeem that promised them.

And so the refugee sighted down the length of his rifle at the alien in his corn and saw justice, and Gideon angled the nose of his jet towards the earth and closed his palm and saw justice in the lethal burden that dropped beneath him.

". . . Rejoice, Children, at the wall of Solomon . . ."

5

One of the few Egyptian planes to fly strikes over the Gaza Strip, a bloody battleground for both Israeli and Arab.

7

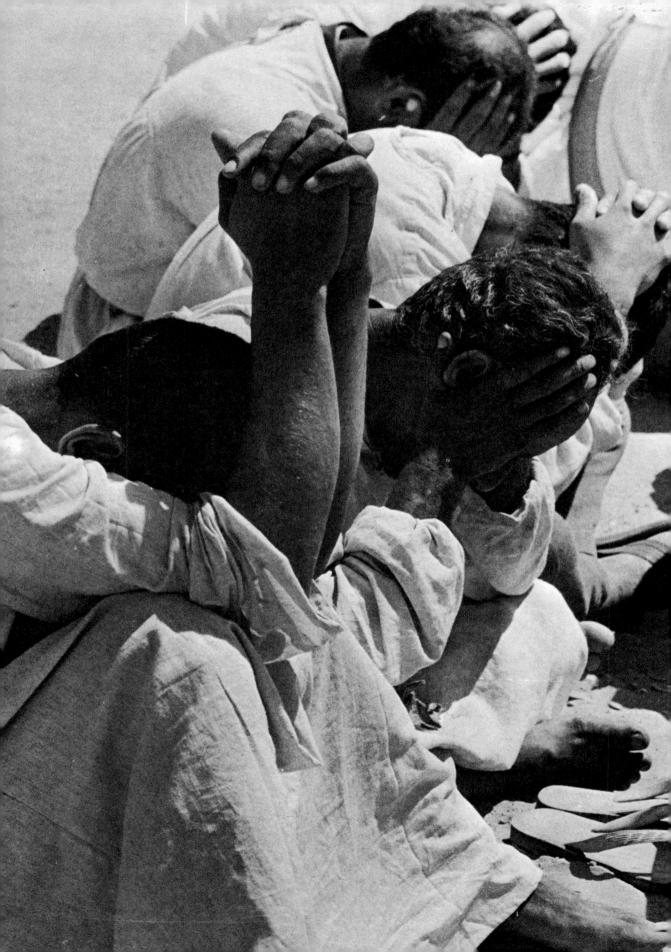

The waste of war, the humility of surrender, the victim of ancient hate.

Jordanian troops drill on the Israeli border just days before the shooting started.

SUNDAY

THE HOSTS ASSEMBLED

■ Sunday in the Middle East is not like Sunday in the Western world. For the Moslems, Friday is the holy day, the day of rest. For the Jews it is Saturday, the Sabbath. For both Arabs and Jews, Sunday, June 4, 1967, was a day of work, a day of watching and wondering and worrying.

In Cairo, on that unseasonably cool Sunday, street vendors were moving in and out among the crowds on Kasr El Nir Street, beneath the anti-American and anti-British banners, shouting: "Blue paper, blue paper, a sheet for two piasters (about five cents)."

Blue paper was a fast moving item now. Every half hour Cairo Radio, in its instructions to the Egyptian people on what to do in case of an air raid, urged covering over windows and automobile headlamps with blue paper as a blackout precaution.

In Tel Aviv, on this hot, humid Sunday, the coffee shops along the Dizengoff, the fashionable main street, were filled with the late theater crowd, and the conversation, as everywhere in Israel, turned excitedly to the latest crisis bulletins coming in over Kol Yisrael, the official Israeli radio. The news was not good. The Cabinet, meeting in the new Knesset building in Jerusalem, had increased income taxes by 10 percent to meet the needs of the emergency. Iraq had just joined Egypt and Jordan in a defense pact. Gamal Abdel Nasser, the fiery president of the United Arab Republic, was still calling for the annihilation of Israel. Tiny Israel was completely encircled by foes.

In Jerusalem, Sunday was cool and pleasant. Tourists sat on the balcony of the King David Hotel listening to the loudspeaker

13

An Egyptian soldier peers across Sinai at Israeli positions.

muezzin call out to Allah from the Mosque of Omar in the Old City, just across the concertinas of barbed wire in Jordan. Nearby, in the winding, picturesque streets of the Mea Shearim, the rigidly Orthodox quarter of new Jerusalem, students from the Talmudic Academy were digging trenches and foxholes, their long black frock coats and long side curls flying with the frenzy of their industry.

The roads leading to all three cities were clogged with long lines of military traffic. From Cairo came the ponderous T-34 and T-54 Russian tanks, clanking down to the Sinai and up to Gaza to join the billion dollars worth of equipment already arrayed along the tense border. From Tel Aviv and Jerusalem, bound for the Negev and the edges of the Gaza, came great convoys of British-made Centurion tanks and American Pattons and Super Shermans, followed by truckloads of confidently waving troops: paratroopers in camouflaged steel helmets, reserves from the kibbutzim (the collective farms) still wearing their pointed-crown hats, pert girl soldiers in khaki miniskirts, cut only recently to a very "mod" length because the army had never got around to deciding on an acceptable hemline.

In the golden hills of Galilee, groves of silver-gray olive groves and the sparkling blue lake on which Christ and His apostles fished seemed to hold time in a changeless trance, like a picture of the Holy Land handed out in Sunday school. Armored tractors moved through the fields, tanks lurked menacingly in orchards of orange and lemon trees, and defense councils in the various border kibbutzim met to decide whether now was the time for the children to go down to the shelters. The kibbutz's first line of defense was already in the trenches, and mechanized infantry units, moved into the area only last week, maneuvered their half-tracks carefully in and out of the wooded areas. As always, they were aware that in Israel every tree had to be purchased and hand-planted in the 20-year miracle of turning the desert into the promised land of milk and honey.

In the bare, yellowish Golan hills, brooding with dismal little Syrian towns, every eucalyptus concealed a tank. The back side of the hills, out of sight of the fertile Israeli valleys below, bristled with antiaircraft guns, howitzers and large Russian mortars, dug into impressive concrete bunkers or lurking behind massive black basaltic boulders in a defense posture that Syria proudly called its "little Maginot Line." In between, the fields of Galilee were a checkerboard of gold and black: gold with the first grain harvest of the season, black where Syrian shells had fallen for the past few weeks in the many battles with the border kibbutzim over disputed lands.

On the windblown sands of the Sinai Desert, where Moses wandered for 40 years, an Egyptian army, awesomely arrayed, dug in its tanks, swatted the voracious desert flies, ran a ready-check on the squadrons of jet fighters strung out on the maintenance lines of the desert airstrips.

All day long Cairo Radio blared out martial music. Every half hour Kol Yisrael interrupted its regular programming with six nervous beeps ushering in a new crisis bulletin. But even with the hysteria and the excitement and the anxiety, life went on in the cities, overlaid here and there with a stark and frequently ludicrous patina of militarism.

The little ladies at the synagogue made cakes for the soldiers camped out in the orange and olive groves. The bloodmobile rolled up in front of Mandy Rice Davis's discotheque on Tel Aviv's Ben Yehudi Street. The fruggers filed up dutifully from that underground pleasure palace, dimly lit with Tiffany glass chandeliers, and took their place on line, Edwardian mod suits and thigh-high miniskirts mingling patriotically with the Orthodox kaftans and exquisitely embroidered Yemenite robes. The old men, watching the paddle ball players on the beaches of Tel Aviv and Herzilya, Nathanya and Ashkelon, wondered, if war came, how the new generation of sabras, the youngsters born in Israel, would react. The feeling was that maybe they had become too soft, too Americanized, too remote from the problems that had faced their pioneer parents in carving a nation out of an unyielding wilderness surrounded by hostile neighbors.

To many of the old-timers, something had gone out of the spirit that made the new state of Israel: immigration had dropped from a peak of a quarter of a million in 1949 to less than 12,000 last year; the rate of growth of the kibbutzim had declined drastically; people were leaving the long-coveted homeland in alarming numbers, some of them doctors and lawyers and scientists, and, for the first time in its 20-year history, the tiny, overtaxed state was troubled with lingering unemployment. On top of all that, the young people were forsaking the old ways, the frug had replaced the hora, the discotheques outdrew the Talmudic classes, and there was increasing grumbling about the dietary laws in the restaurants and the lack of bus service on the Sabbath.

The war spirit, at least, was drawing the people together again, reminding them of their beginnings and the ancient yearnings for the holy places always tantalizingly in sight but separated by rows of Jordanian barbed wire.

Youngsters took over the jobs of the men —18 to 49—who had left for the army. They worked as mailmen and mail sorters. Boys and girls on bicycles delivered the mail.

Civil Defense officials ordered homeowners to clear out their basements for use as air raid shelters. High school boys took the jobs of garbagemen to cart away the trash.

Young men were a rare sight on the streets.

In Cairo, there was a feeling of confidence, even cockiness. Nasser's boldness in closing the Straits of Tiran and facing down the United Nations had won the admiration of the masses, filling them with the hope of righting ancient wrongs. The voice of Palestine Radio in Cairo was calling on the Jordanians to "turn the Mandelbaum Gate into a Second Tiran." Now, at last, after years of bickering, the Arab leaders were bonded together in brotherhood, and

Nasser would lead them, so that the Arab world would again hold the entire Mediterranean in the palm of its hand and ancient Palestine would be returned to the dispossessed, the more than one million refugees waiting for nearly two decades in drab United Nations camps to go home.

The thought of an Egyptian army camped on the Sinai only a few miles from the borders of Israel excited the crowds in the streets. The army had grown mightily since 1956, and national pride cried out for vengeance for the surprise attack against the unprepared forces that had been beaten back in the Sinai 11 years before.

In Amman and Cairo, Damascus and the Old City of Jerusalem, Arab housewives wondered how long the war would last and whether they should store some flour or cheese or maybe potatoes. In Egypt, where the entire nation lives on only two meat days a week, there would surely be shortages.

In Israel, where 2.5 million people were surrounded by 110 million Arab enemies, arrayed on every border, patience was running out with the plodding efforts of the diplomats and Nasser's rising invective.

And in Israel time was running out. Mobilization was costing the tiny country $15 to $20 million a day in lost production in factories and fields because the men had gone off to military duty. She could not afford to wait while the diplomats negotiated. Three months of mobilization could wreck her economy.

"What's the good of waiting?" asked a European-born army officer, a regular who had been to Sinai in 1956 and fought for independence in 1948. "Time is against us. Nasser said he seeks to destroy us. Why shouldn't we believe him?"

■ On this Sunday night, Colonel Mohamed Galal, 41, commander of an Egyptian artillery brigade, felt things were going smoothly in his stretch of the Sinai. His men and guns had taken up position two days before in Wadi el Arish. Now they stood only 37 miles from the border of Israel and the night was quiet. A thin haze blurred the moon slightly but the desert sky was, as ever, a splendor of stars.

Last night Colonel Galal had talked with Laila, his wife, by phone. From their home in Beni Suef, on the bank of the Nile 250 miles to the west, she reported that everything was fine, their four children were well and Terek, 13 and the eldest, couldn't wait to get on the line.

"Poppa, I passed my exams with an 89.5

Israeli tankers drill in the south of Israel.

average! I succeeded, poppa. You owe me the money."

The colonel's son had been promised a reward if he exceeded an average of 80.

"All right, I'll send you the money."

Laila returned to the phone and reported that the baby, an 18-month-old girl, was sleeping soundly. And it was time to say good-bye and the wife back in Egypt said to her colonel in the Sinai: "I wish you good luck."

Now, on Sunday evening, Colonel Galal met with his staff. Their reports indicated everything was going routinely; the morale of the men, they said, was high.

"Are we going to fight?" asked a new lieutenant, fresh from officer's school.

"We are standing in defensive positions," the colonel said.

"Why are we waiting?"

The colonel, a veteran of 20 years in the army, a tall, trim man with olive skin and

17

handsome mustache, looked evenly at the eager young officer and made no answer.

At 10, Galal decided to turn in. Heading for his lorry, his eyes automatically swept over his position, over his 700 men and his 36 guns. The guns were Russian-made howitzers. Half of them were new. All of them faced east.

The brigade occupied low ground south of the road from Bir Hasana to El Quseima. Ahead of it stood another line of Egyptian soldiers and guns, between Galal and Israel. On his left was a mechanized infantry brigade and beyond it, a mountain. On his right, another mechanized infantry brigade and, again, a mountain.

To his back, out of sight beyond high ground, was Bir Hasana, which consisted of a police station and a few houses clustered around a well.

Having swept the scene full circle and satisfied with what he saw, Mohamed Galal climbed into the back of his lorry, stretched out on a mattress and was soon asleep. He slept without dreams this last night of peace.

As usual, he awoke at 5 A.M., on Monday, June 5. He shaved from a plastic basin in the lorry and stepped outside into the cool, predawn desert, wearing his heavy coat for the chill. He walked down to the gun positions, inspected the weapons, talked to the men.

Satisfied with what he saw and heard, Mohamed Galal returned from the line for breakfast with the other officers. It was now only 8:30 A.M. but already the sun was hot. They ate at a table moved into the limited shade of a desert bush. They drank hot tea and ate boiled eggs, cheese, flat round bread, jam and fresh apricots. A man couldn't ask for more, at 8:30 A.M., Monday, June 5.

■ Corporal Kamal Mahrouss* had been at El Kuntilla, 50 miles southeast of Colonel Galal's position in the Sinai, for 14 days

King Hussein visits the Israel border and is briefed on the military situation.

18

now. Or was it 15? Kamal knew today's date—Sunday, June 4—but the emptiness of the desert and the tedium of army routine had a way of erasing the memory of each passing day. Anyway, it didn't matter. What mattered was that the division was ready, dug in solid, guns pointed east, aimed straight at the border of Israel. But Corporal Kamal Mahrouss was impatient.

Kamal, 24-year-old professional soldier, had come to the Sinai to fight for Egypt and for Nasser but so far had done nothing but dig trenches. He had come, indeed, to die for Egypt and for Nasser, if death were asked of him. Such was the devotion of Kamal Mahrouss to his country and his president. Had not Nasser given Kamal's poor father five acres of good land, some goats and a buffalo in the agrarian reform? And was not Kamal pure Egyptian? "Yes, praise God, and pure Moslem."

The days were long and lonely and the recent past obscure, but Kamal Mahrouss would not easily forget the day his trip to El Kuntilla began.

It was May 15, a Monday, when his infantry division got the word it would be pulling out. Nobody knew where, or why. Rumors were plentiful, as always, but likely wrong. Next morning, in full battle dress, they began rolling north. They passed the great pyramids of Giza and lumbered on into Cairo. The people gawked and some cheered as the big trucks and half-tracks shouldered through the crowded streets. Then the column turned east, toward Suez. There it halted.

What now? Again, only rumors. Finally the order came: The column would cross the Canal into the Sinai. War with Israel at last? Kamal danced and sang and embraced his companions and they embraced him and everyone laughed and shouted. "God is great! Long live Nasser! Long live Nasser!"

Kamal held his rifle to his lips and kissed it. Overhead fighter planes in crisp formations traced patterns in the sky. And Kamal thought, "The land and skies of God belong to nobody but us. We are invincible. We can overrun Israel in a matter of hours."

But on this night, June 4, the intoxica-tion of that moment seemed long ago. Why do we wait so long? Will the war never begin? Corporal Kamal Mahrouss drew up his blanket and closed his eyes and awaited the dawn.

■ On Sunday afternoon, Captain Matan Goor and the other members of the 55th Parachute Battalion were encamped in a dusty field near the Lod Airport, Israel's big passenger jet field that lies between Tel Aviv and Jerusalem. They had been there for twelve days, since May 23, when "the crisis," as most of them still called it, summoned them from reserve to active duty.

Toward evening Goor got orders to pack up and move. He loaded his men into air-conditioned tourist buses, which only a few days ago had been taking rich Americans and Canadians to Nazareth and Tiberias, and settled back to an hour-long ride over clogged, convoy-crawling roads to Tel Nov, a military jet field, near the town of Rehovoth. This time they made camp in an orange grove. Goor, a handsome, blue-eyed veteran of nearly 17 years service in the reserves and dozens of actions against the Egyptians, Syrians and Jordanians, was happy with the layout. His men would have some shade for a change, under the citrus trees, and some fruit for plucking. One of his men, a ser-geant named Mordy, even managed to sneak into the nearby airfield and get a phone call through to Goor's wife at their home in Pardess Hana, a coastal town between Tel Aviv and Haifa.

"I told her you were all right and there was nothing to worry about," Mordy re-ported. "She says the children are fine but she is still convinced there will be war."

Goor smiled at his wife's pessimism and was grateful for Mordy's report.

The captain brewed a pot of tea on his little primus stove and settled down to con-template the familiar academic skyline of Rehovoth, with the towers and rooftops of its Agricultural Research Center rising out of the twilight haze. It was here that he had

met his handsome wife, dark-eyed Simcha, when they were both students at the Agriculture Center, and it was here that they had first been summoned to active duty in the 1956 war. She went as an airplane spotter in the Air Force, he as a parachute lieutenant, who wound up fighting at Nakhl and the Mitla Pass in the central Sinai Peninsula.

That first time, when he was a student at the agricultural center, they had sent a messenger to the house at 7 o'clock in the morning. This time, he was on his way to the Agricultural Secondary School in Pardess Hana, where he taught biology and served as vice-principal, when a telephone call told him to stand by for a call to active duty. Goor figured it wouldn't be long in coming. Most of his friends in town already were heading off for duty.

That day, Tuesday, May 23, he taught school, as usual, and even had an evening class that ended at 5 P.M. When he got home at 5:30 P.M., a staff car was waiting to take him off.

His wife, also a teacher, in a school for problem children—mostly the emotionally disturbed children of divorced parents—was certain there would be war. He felt the exact opposite and was sure that Nasser was only bluffing.

Their two boys, 9-year-old Yehuda and 5-year-old Gideon, didn't cry or show any particular emotion when he left. They had seen him go off so often before; this time didn't look any different. Their mother, who hated war and violence, never permitted them to play soldiers or read about war. They wanted to be cowboys, not soldiers, and Captain Goor was just as happy.

He belonged to a special "reaction unit" that was called out at all sorts of hours on all sorts of assignments, like making lightning raids into Jordan or Syria, whenever the "fedayun," the Arab underground terrorist organization, stuck an Israeli kibbutz or shot up a produce truck on the road.

At 35, Goor was a bit old to be a paratrooper, and so were most of his men. All of them had signed waiver papers enabling them to keep their paratroop wings and not have to join the "stiff legs," the infantry. Looking at them now, gathered at small cook fires and resting under the orange trees, the captain felt a surge of pride for his men. They had been together, most of them, for nearly 17 years, meeting for 30 days each year at summer camp or on duty at the border, and oftener than that when a reprisal action was ordered. He thought it odd that they never met in civilian life and yet enjoyed a close bond of friendship, closer than among his civilian friends, from their frequent meetings in arms.

Like most of his men, Goor had been born in Israel. He was a sabra, named for the desert cactus, "prickly on the outside, sweet on the inside." He was born in Jerusalem, where his father worked in the agricultural ministry. It was his grandfather, a fervent Zionist, who brought the family to Israel 85 years ago, changing the family name from Grazowsky to Goor. Grandfather Jude Grazowsky, later Goor, was a renowned Hebrew scholar who wrote a famous Hebrew-Russian dictionary—"Goor's Dictionary"—that was still a standard work in the schools and colleges.

Captain Goor's thoughts turned to Simcha again, and he wondered if she would ever stop worrying about war. She, too, was a sabra, he was proud to recall, the daughter of "pioneers," founders of the state, who had migrated from Poland 32 years ago. Her father, a building contractor in Pardess Hana, literally had helped build the country and had seen it grow from a windswept desert to the promised land of milk and honey. Simcha, though several years younger than Goor, was no longer in the air force reserves. But she would have her hands full, running the family and taking on an extra-heavy load at school, now that most of the other teachers had gone off.

The captain looked across at the airfield, where a tank column was taking up positions along the main jet runway. He noticed that the crews were camouflaging their British Centurion tanks with olive branches. He thought it was a good omen.

A thin scrim of clouds spread across the star-studded night, giving the cobalt Medi-

Barbed wire in the Holy City frames the Church of the Dormition in Jordan, as seen from Israel.

terranean sky a soothing, diaphanous look. Captain Goor curled up in his blanket roll, more than ever convinced that there would be no war.

■ Across the border from Jerusalem, in Jordan, war seemed inevitable to Mohammed Ibn Jamil.

"They were occupying our land and we could never forget it," he said.

He was only 39. But he had been fighting Jews off and on for 19 years. He was the warrior son of a warrior father of a warrior people and he looked it. Tall. Mustachioed. Strong. Black eyes and black hair. He could have played one of the Arab leads in *Lawrence of Arabia*.

But Jamil was no Hollywood caricature. He was a major in one of the world's most romantic armies, the Arab Legion.

Jamil was of the Beni Sakhr tribe, whose domain reached over 6,000 square miles of desert west of Amman. Their name—"sons of the rock"—told much of these people. They were said to be "the rock on which all attacks foundered."

In the wastes of their desert home these Bedouins had developed an elaborate and sincerely felt courtesy in the goat-hair tents in which they lived. And they had developed a great ferocity in their endless battles over the sands.

Until his death two months before, the Beni Sakhr had been led by Mithgal Pasha el Fayez, a fierce patriarch who had died at 95 still bearing the sword wound he suffered fighting the Turks with T. E. Lawrence. El Fayez had been instrumental in installing King Abdullah, Hussein's grandfather, as King of Jordan. Once he had captured 100 British soldiers who had come to take taxes from his tribe and tied their commander to a horse in his stable for three days rather than accept British domination.

El Fayez had bowed to change enough to build a concrete home for his two wives and children. But he himself lived in a black goat-hair tent nearby. Up until his death he rode his horse every day and

every day he drank a bucket of camel's milk. Of such people was Major Jamil.

He and his infantry battalion had moved into Jordanian Jerusalem as soon as the crisis broke out. They took up positions behind vicious coils of barbed wire and dug trenches in the ancient earth just on the Jordan side of the no-man's-land that divided the city. On his left, Jamil's lines reached down to the Damascus Gate into the Old City. In the Old City itself, behind the walls, the narrow alleys hardly wide enough for a donkey to squeeze through, tank warfare was all but impossible. But Jamil's men were in a newer part of the city. His lines ran along a wide road that skirted no-man's-land and up into the comfortable residences of the American colony and the Ambassador Hotel, the American and British consulates and the Y.M.C.A.

The Arab Legion had held this land in 1948 against Jewish attack, the only Arabs to turn back the Israelis. Jamil was confident his men could do so again. In 1965 they had fought well in a two-hour skirmish with an Israeli patrol at the village of Umm el Rihan, north of Jenin and right on the border. They would fight well again. If they had to.

The Arab Legion was a direct descendant of Lawrence and many of its men, such as Jamil, were direct descendants of men who fought with him. In the days of empire, Britain wanted a force that would keep the peace in lands so close to her oil and canal. So, largely at British initiative, Transjordan was created out of tribal desert land after World War I and the rulers set about creating an army of its nomadic Bedouins, legendary descendants of the Moabites, who the Bible says lost 10,000 men to the Children of Israel led by the left-handed commander, Ehud.

For all the days of their years these Bedouins had fought, themselves and others. After the war they were plagued by the Wahabis, religious fanatics from Saudi Arabia. The British formed them into an army, really the creature of one man, Sir John Bagot Glubb—Glubb Pasha. A professional soldier son of a professional soldier,

Glubb, who was a friend of Lawrence, had fought in World War I, later left the army for an administrative job in the government being formed in Iraq from the ruins of the Ottoman Empire. He eventually came to Transjordan.

King Abdullah asked if he had travelled by car from Baghdad. No, Glubb said, by camel.

"By the Prophet," the King exclaimed, "he is a true Bedouin!" And he was. Glubb lived among the Arabs, slept in their tents and ate camel and goat with them with his fingers. He always carried Moslem prayer beads. Wherever he was, large crowds of Arabs would gather to tell him their problems and ask him to judge their disputes. They called him *Abu Hainak,* "Father of the Little Chin," because part of his jaw had been shot away in World War I.

Glubb had started with 100 Bedouins who wore red and white headdresses and flowing Arab robes. They wore their hair long, earning them the mocking name of "Glubb's girls." But they were sure shots, tough and deft with the *khanjar,* the curved knife they wore in their belts. They became a first-rate fighting force. They brought peace to a land that had successfully resisted Roman, Crusader and Turk. In Glubb's early days tribes were still raiding each other, now in Cadillacs and Chevrolets. Glubb put an end to this, his Legionnaires now in jeeps and tanks. A nation took shape.

The Legion fought with the British in World War II. It held the Old City for Islam in 1948. Jamil had been with them, his men on guard on the hills above the road from Jaffa to Jerusalem. Once his men ambushed an Israeli command car, killing an officer and four soldiers. Jamil was proud of his men.

He was only 20 then. He had been a cadet for six months, enrolled by personal order of King Abdullah. "I didn't want to join the army because all the officers were British. But the royal decree was a command. I obeyed."

It is one of the paradoxes of this contradictory land that the Legion, a creature of the British, should do battle with Israel, in large part also a creature of Britain. After the '48 war, Jamil, who had no stomach for the British, resigned and returned to his family's farm.

Then, in 1956, Glubb was dismissed by young King Hussein who wanted to Arabize the officer corps. Glubb had also argued that the Legion's strategy dictated a withdrawal to the west bank of the Jordan River in the event of an attack by the more numerous Israelis. Hussein said no. The Arabs had already lost too much of their land to the infidel.

So the British went. How would their leaving affect the Legion? The Bedouin soldiers remained loyal to their king. But many of the officers, Palestinian refugees not of the desert, were susceptible to intrigue against Hussein. The King, who had been at Abdullah's side when the old king was assassinated, personally drove to the Legion camp once to put down a coup aimed at his throne.

With the British gone, Jamil had rejoined the Legion in 1957. He had attended a training session in tank warfare at Fort Knox in the United States. This son of the desert knew modern warfare. He knew his men could fight, would fight to regain their land. He also knew that for all their tanks and cannon, the Jordanian army was not a fully rounded force.

The Legionnaires had machine guns—and their silver-scabbarded knives. But they had only a handful of jet fighters. Was that enough?

■ Jericho on this first Sunday in June was a lazy, lovely, nearly deserted city. Christian Arabs, relaxing on their sabbath, sat in the shade of the olive trees in the sun-drenched city square, talking excitedly over a game of shesh-besh, an ancient form of checkers played with pebbles. The hot breath of the hamsin, the sultry desert wind, blew in from the Dead Sea, five miles to the south. In the distance, above its turquoise salt-flecked waters, the Mountains of Moab shimmered in the heat rising from

Arab volunteers in Jordan await equipment and orders.

the arid plain that seemed to stretch end-lessly into the Negev.

But Jericho, at 825 feet below sea level, was, as it had been in the day of Herod the Great, "fair as a garden of the Lord," an oasis of brilliant red flowers, lush banana and date groves. Here, wealthy Arab bankers and businessmen built their winter villas, escaping from the chilling winds and rain that swept Jerusalem and Amman, to a breathlessly beautiful setting of lawns and courtyards, palm trees and rose gardens, irrigated by the same great underground spring that had watered the famous gardens of Herod's winter palace 2,000 years ago.

But it was summer now. Most of the big hotels, sprawling villas and exclusive *pen-sions* were closed, and Jericho's population had dropped from its seasonal peak of 42,000 to less than 5,000. Only one sight-seeing bus came down from Amman this Sunday, full of Scandinavian tourists. They scrambled happily about the archaeological excavations of what the guides insisted was the oldest walled city in the world although they were reticent about whether they were

the actual walls that fell to Joshua's trumpets.

If Jericho itself was nearly deserted, the main road on the edge of town to Jerusalem was a constant confusion of military traffic that left a long cloud of dust hanging in the dry, hot air. At Aqabat Jaber, a refugee camp a few miles out of town, Rashid Areikat, a thin, sad-eyed Arab in his 40's, sat in a tubular chair in the shaded portico outside his office watching the tanks roll by.

Tanks and half-tracks had been moving down the highway in the direction of Jerusalem for several days now, ever since King Hussein went to Cairo to confer with President Nasser. But now for the first time, he noticed that the really big stuff, American-built Pershings and Super Shermans, was clanking by, most of it painted in the dun-nish yellow colors of the Iraqi army instead of Jordan's olive drab.

Areikat was deputy area officer for the United Nations Relief and Works Agency (UNRWA) in charge of more than 50,000 Palestinian refugees in four camps: three on the west bank of the Jordan, one on the east bank, all within a few miles of Jericho.

He was certain that there would be no war, despite the constant, dusty clatter along the road, but he was worried about the rising expectations and tensions among the refugees.

Usually his problems were fewer at the beginning of the month, when the camp dwellers received their slender monthly rations from UNRWA: 10 kilograms of flour, 500 grams of sugar, 500 grams of rice, 950 grams of beans, one cake of soap. Now, there was more grumbling than usual about the food, and more and more in the past few days his people were getting up their hopes over Nasser, looking upon him as the saviour who would deliver them out of their bondage of longing and waiting. Nearly half of the refugees had been born in the prefab camps under Areikat's care, but the other half, the older half, had been waiting nearly 20 years to go home, home to what they still considered Israeli-occupied Palestine. Nasser's perpetual invective and rash promises of wiping out the State of Israel in the past few days struck many of them as a more promising course of action than their own young king's temporizing.

"Hussein is an affable child," Areikat heard one of his storehouse clerks telling those on line who were waiting for rations. "Nasser will give him some backbone. Then we will all be out of here at last."

Fortunately most of the younger hotheads had gone off from the camp; some to work the summer harvests in Samaria, "Hussein's grain belt," some to join the Arab Legion. But even those who went off to join the Legion did so for the same reason as the harvest workers, to augment their income. Few among the refugees could raise a family on the rations handed out by UNRWA, especially since those born in the camps after 1951 were not, by UN agreement, eligible for rations.

All day long, the tanks filed by, along the same road that Pompey's legions had taken, along the same road out of Jericho where Jesus of Nazareth had cured the two blind men who cried out, "Lord, that I may see."

Rashid Areikat got into his small automobile and drove across the Allenby Bridge to Karameh, his farthest camp on the other side of the Jordan, 22 miles to the northeast.

■ Farther up the Jordan River, the ruling council of Kibbutz Ein Gev was meeting in the dining room on this same Sunday. The council decided that the Middle East crisis had become so serious it was time for action. They ordered all the children to go to the shelter. There was no panic, no crying, no kissing and waving good-bye as the children went off. Even the two- and three-year-olds toddled off without any display of emotion. With old experienced kibbutz-niks like Benjamin Ben-Yosef and Gershon Fine teasing them and kidding them along the way, the little ones filed past the empty concert hall and went down the concrete steps leading to the huge shelter hidden beneath a pleasant mound covered with rhododendrons in full bloom.

For Kibbutz Ein Gev, on the eastern shore of the Sea of Galilee one and a half miles from the Syrian border, the war had begun a long time ago. Ten times in recent years heavy shelling from the Syrian emplacements on the Golan hills had driven all 400 members of the kibbutz into their trenches and shelters.

Less than two months ago, on April 7, the Syrians took offense because Tel Kazir, the neighboring kibbutz, began tilling some fields in a disputed area of the demilitarized zone near the border. They opened up with Russian-made mortars, killing 10 good milk cows in Kibbutz Ein Gev, knocking down a classroom used for Hebrew studies and hitting several cottages and apartments, including the doctor's house. One shell landed near the concert hall and defaced the "Widow's Statue." This was a memorial to a woman who carried on after her husband was killed in the War of Independence, when regular units from the Syrian and Iraqi armies overran a pillbox at the gates of the kibbutz but failed to push the doughty defenders back into the sea.

The shelling in April of this year kept the citizens of Ein Gev in the shelter for more than two hours. Then Israeli jets came streaking across the sapphire-blue waters of the Sea of Galilee, where Christ and His apostles used to fish, and strafed the gun emplacements in the barren yellow hills. In two and a half minutes, the guns were silenced, the jets were heading home and the members of Kibbutz Ein Gev were heading out into the fields again.

For Kibbutz Ein Gev, crisis was a normal way of life. Only the old-timers, the founding fathers as they were called, could recall a time when they didn't have to plow with one eye on the furrow and the other on the Syrian heights. Only the old-timers could remember when Ein Gev's sardine fleet, a main source of kibbutz revenue, could drop its nets in the northeast corner of the lake (where the fishing is best because that is where the River Jordan flows in) without being fired on by Syrian gunboats.

Over the years, the Syrians kept the communal dwellers so busy and on the alert that they long ago did away with the weekly shelter drill. They went to the shelter so often, no practice was needed.

Kibbutz Ein Gev, accustomed to constant crisis, lived with but one dream. It wanted to build a hotel, like some of the more prosperous kibbutzim in the south, and hang out a sign, "Diners Club, American Express Cards Welcome," to attract the rich American tourists. But security conditions never permitted them to let the idea go beyond the planning stage.

The kibbutz is a purely Israeli phenomenon, an experiment in rural, communal living that has drawn the attention of sociologists the world over. The word kibbutz (plural: kibbutzim) means collective. It is a voluntary, democratic society, functioning through a series of committees that govern the community, assign the work, harvest and sell the goods raised by the members. The group takes care of the members every need, including raising and educating the children. There is no private property. There are more than 200 kibbutzim in Israel with a total membership of 100,000.

Kibbutz Ein Gev, a green, pleasant place with its own fishing fleet, a fine fish restaurant, groves of bananas and dates, had been wrested from the desert by courageous immigrant Jews from western Europe and the Baltic states. Most of the pioneer settlers who arrived in 1937 had never done a day's work by hand in their lives. They were *yeckes*—the jacketed ones—bourgeois Jews from middle-class urban families, who learned to farm and fish and raise chickens and irrigate, so that their toil and sweat and dedication turned an arid, unyielding soil into one of the lushest valleys in all of Israel.

For 10 years, the founders of Ein Gev, concentrating mainly on raising bananas and fishing for sardines in the lake where Christ wrought His miracle of the multiplication of the fishes, labored in relative peace and security. Then the British Mandate ended abruptly in 1948 and the War of Independence began. Clinging to a strip of shoreline between the water's edge and the heavily-fortified heights, Ein Gev held out against repeated attacks by Syrian and Iraqi regulars. At night the children were evacuated across the lake by fishing boat, along with the cattle and the chickens. In the final assault, the embattled *yeckes* of Ein Gev fought for their land and their lives at hand-to-hand range, falling back from their pillbox and watchtower at the gates, to make a last successful stand just a few hundred feet from the lake.

From that day on, Kibbutz Ein Gev never knew a day's peace and security. They went to the fields in armored tractors, huge, lumbering, tanklike monsters. Their fishermen were killed, their produce convoys ambushed on the narrow road to Tiberias, the nearest market.

Under the terms of the armistice that ended the 1948 war, the kibbutz land fell mainly within a demilitarized zone, which meant the members could not build fortifications to defend themselves against the frequent shellings from the Golan hills. Still, the community prospered. Its concert hall, built with the help of United States Point Four funds, was one of the great tourist attractions of the Galilee area, a sort of Tanglewood East, to which on Passover came such international stars as Marion Anderson, Sir Thomas Beecham, the Martha Graham Dancers, Yehudi Menuin. This year the attraction was Margot Fonteyn and the Royal Ballet, and as usual the kibbutz sent word to the Syrian Embassy that foreign stars would be on hand and that any shelling might result in an international incident. Ein Gev was always nervous about its big cultural attractions, which brought visitors from all over Israel. The concert hall, with its marvelous acoustics, held 2,500 people; the shelter beneath the rhododendrons, with its cots and lamps and stores of water and food, held only a few hundred under what the council called "situation sardine." But when the Syrians saw the lights on in the concert hall and the long line of cars streaming down the road from Tiberias, they always held their fire.

When the Middle East crisis warmed up again in May, Ein Gev had just completed another of its Ulpan programs, which brought Jewish and gentile students from all over the world for a six-month course in Hebrew. Under the plan, the students worked four hours a day around the kibbutz and studied for four hours. Since April 7, when the Hebrew classroom took a direct mortar hit on the roof, classes were held in the fish restaurant overlooking the lake. Although the course was over, eleven of the students decided to stay on, to see Kibbutz Ein Gev through the crisis. Among them were a Canadian, two Germans, a Frenchman and an American girl, all gentiles. The girl, Nancy Donaught of Washington, D.C., had received $500 from her parents to come home immediately when things began to warm up in the Gulf of Aqaba, but she wired back, "I am frightened to death but I cannot go away at a time like this and abandon my friends."

Still, most of the 250 adult kibbutzniks were confirmed "peaceniks," as Gershon Fine called them. Nearly half of them had lost all of their families in German concentration camps, and war was the last thing they wanted. Fine's family had been driven out of Russia into Manchuria by one of the Czarist pogroms. He met his wife, a nurse, at Ein Gev, during the 1948 war. She proudly wore on her arm the indelible tattoo of the concentration camp at Rosenheim, Germany, where she spent a year and barely escaped the gas chambers.

Gershon Fine, a tanned, heavy man with the kindly look of a country doctor, breathed heavily as a result of asthma.

"There will be no war, Esther," he said to her, as they escorted the young ones down to the shelter that Sunday night. "Maybe a little shelling, but in this civilized day and age, who wants war? The big powers and the UN would never let it happen."

Up the road a few miles to the west along the lake shore, Kibbutz Degania, "the Mother of Kibbutzim," which Moshe Dayan's father had helped found in 1909 and to which Ben-Gurion belonged, was similarly buckling down. Communal life was geared for constant crisis: the children were going to the shelter, the men to the ditches and bunkers, the women to the kitchen to prepare standby rations.

All of this where the Galilean had stood on the shores of the same lake and told the crowds seated on a little grassy mount: "Blessed are the peacemakers: For they shall be called the children of God."

A nightingale swooped down and plucked at the grapes growing near the entrance to Kibbutz Ein Gev. It lifted its head and delivered its sweet song.

"It will come to nothing," Gershon Fine said to Benjamin Ben-Yosef. "Nasser is preening himself for the benefit of the other Arab leaders."

Darkness fell amid a glory of stars, and a thin moon rose over the bleak Golan heights.

One could almost look at the dark shadows and see the ghosts of past warriors who had fought over those antique hills. So many ghosts . . .

*Kamal Mahrouss and Mohammed Ibn Jamil are fictional names. The men and their experiences are real. In telling their stories to correspondents of The Associated Press, these two men asked that their true names be withheld for their own protection. These are the only fictional names in this book.

TYRE •

MA'LULA • *One of three villages where ancient language is still spoken*

ACRE

80,000 crusaders died besieging the city in the 12th century.

HORNS OF HATTON
Sermon on the mount

SEA OF GALILEE

NAZARETH

Home of Jesus

CAESAREA •
Headquarters of Pontius Pilate during the Roman rule.

SALIM •

JERASH •

Jacob's well

John baptized here

Site of the ancient Gerasa

SYCHAR •

JERICHO •

JERUSALEM •

Dead Sea Scrolls

BETHLEHEM •

MACHAREUS •

Where John The Baptist was beheaded

GAZA •

David slew Goliath

John The Baptist preached here in the wilderness of Judaea

HALUTSA •

NITSANA •

SHIVTA •

AVDAT •

Ancient crossing used by The Holy Family fleeing from Herod

Prosperous Nabatean towns

TIMNA •
Site of King Solomon's copper mines

MOUNT SINAI

Moses received the Ten Commandments

The land of Abraham and the sons of Abraham. The land of Jesus and of Mohammed, of Tamerlane and of Saladin and Richard the Lion Hearted... framed in today's bloody boundaries.

THE SEED OF ABRAHAM

And so it had come to pass that the cohorts of Zion, Egypt and Arabia would do battle yet again in the land of their fathers.

Each had taken the land many times, in their turn. But none had held it, not forever. Nor had they ever left it, not completely.

They were all cousins, children of Abraham. But they had rarely been brothers.

They claimed the land as promised of their Gods—Jehovah and Allah—and had raised temples to them, side by side and one upon the ruins of another, and this had forever riven them.

Their Gods had pledged them a land of milk and honey. Too often it had been of blood. And so it would be again, as the Egyptian—Mohamed Galal—and the Arab—Mohammed Ibn Jamil—and the Hebrew—Matan Goor—came forth for battle as rank upon rank had come before them.

. . . Sennacherib, the Assyrian, had come, "his cohorts all gleaming in purple and gold," and his descendants had scattered the 10 tribes of Israel to the nameless winds of history . . . Nebuchadnezzar of Babylon had come, and had put the Hebrew into a fiery furnace as another would do many centuries later . . . Alexander the Great had come, and granted the Jews religious freedom . . . Judah Maccabee had come, and won the land from those of Greece who would have had his people bow down before Zeus in the Temple of Jerusalem. . . . Marc Antony had come, and for centuries the land would know the might of Imperial Rome. . . . Titus, the Roman, had come, and burned the Temple and driven its defenders down the paths of time that would lead to the ghettos of many alien lands. . . . The hawk-nosed men of the desert had come, and claimed the land for Allah. . . . Richard the Lion Heart had come carrying the cross and sword of Christendom, and done battle with Saladin, the Kurd, who also had come. . . . And the Mamelukes, the slave kings of Egypt, had come, and Timur the Lame, the Mongol known as Tamerlane, had come, and the Turk called the Ottoman had come, and Napoleon had come, and Sir Edmund Allenby had come, trembling the ancient earth with its last great cavalry charge. . . . So had they all come: Hyksos and Jebusites and Hittites and Canaanites and Philistines and Assyrian and Babylonian and Roman and Seljuk and they were gone now and there remained only two, the Hebrew, one of the first to come, and the Arab, who had long been there. Each said the land was theirs by faith and by history and they were both right and there was no Solomon to give them justice. So the children of Abraham would have blood, each of the other.

■ Begin with Abraham.

The Bible says he came from the Chaldean city of Ur, a vanished city in what is now Iraq. It was sometime in the second millenium before Christ. God spoke to Abraham and made a covenant, promising his seed the land "from the river of Egypt to the great river, the river Euphrates."

God reaffirmed the covenant to Abraham's son, Isaac ". . . for unto thee, and unto thy seed, I will give all these countries. . . ." But Abraham had another son, Ishmael, born to Hagar, the handmaid of Abraham's wife, Sarah.

Of Ishmael, God told Abraham: "I have blessed him and will make him fruitful and will multiply him exceedingly, twelve princes shall he beget and I will make him a great nation. But my covenant I will establish with Isaac."

This the Hebrews believe. But the Koran says "And when Abraham said, 'My Lord, make this a land secure and provide its people with fruits, such of them as believe in God and the Last Day,' He said 'and whoso disbelieve, to him I shall give enjoyment a little and then I shall compel him to the chastisement of the Fire'—how evil a homecoming!"

And this the Moslem Arabs believe, tracing their line through Ishmael, the nomadic son of Abraham.

The sons of Isaac and the sons of Ishmael have both ruled the land. The first Hebrew king, Saul, who lived about 1000 B.C., established an empire that, in the time of David, was to reach from the Euphrates to the Gulf of Aqaba. The northern half of the kingdom, Israel, was annihilated by the Assyrians under Sargon in 722. In 586 B.C. Nebuchadnezzar overran Judah, the surviving part of the dual kingdom. He sacked Jerusalem, burned Solomon's great temple, and took the Hebrews into captivity. The diaspora, the scattering of the surviving tribes of Israel, had begun. Cyrus, the Persian, would later permit the Hebrews to return to their homeland. Some of the wealthy Jews preferred to stay in Babylon but gave money to finance the return of others, just as rich Zionists were to do many centuries later.

In 322 B.C. Ptolemy I of Egypt conquered Jerusalem, striking on the Sabbath as would the Arabs against the Jewish kibbutzim in another age. Israel knew independence again in the second century before Christ when a Jewish priest, Mattathais, slew a Hellenic official who demanded he worship Greek gods in his temple.

In 66 A.D. the Jews revolted again, this time against Rome, after the Imperial Protector, Florus, seized the vestments of the High Priest during a Passover celebration and demanded payment from the Temple fund. Caesar had conquered Gaul with 25,000 legionnaires. Titus, son of the Emperor Vespasian, needed 80,000 to reduce Jerusalem. He burned the Temple, threw children into the flames, and sent the survivors into bondage. Tacitus estimates 600,000 people were slain. Among them was a small band at Masada who, cut off by the Romans, put all their families to death and then drew lots to pick those who would kill the surviving men down to the last one. He cut his own throat.

They built a triumphal arch in honor of Titus's victory in Rome. It still stands. But, unwittingly, the Romans had built something else. During Titus's siege of Jerusalem,

Rabbi Jochanan ben Zakki had himself smuggled out of the city in a coffin into the Roman camp to ask permission to establish a yeshiva in the country to study the ancient Hebrew scriptures. His request was granted. So, while the Romans herded the people of Israel away, the faith abided, both on its native soil in the seeds of Ben Zakki's yeshiva and in the Bible that became a portable homeland for the Jews.

There was one last wrench by the few Jews who remained in Israel. In 132 A.D. Bar Kochba ("Son of the Star") led a revolt against Hadrian. His ill-fated band was to be the last Jewish army for almost 2,000 years.

Meanwhile, other armies came to the Holy Land. Omar, a successor to Mohammed, captured Jerusalem for Islam. There the Moslems built a mosque, the Dome of the Rock, where they said Abraham had prepared to sacrifice Isaac and where Mohammed, by tradition, ascended to heaven on his steed, Borak. Along with Mecca, where the faithful believe Abraham and Ishmael are buried, the Dome of the Rock became a holy place.

Mohammed had formed a great faith carried across much of the Middle East and along the Mediterranean littoral by the swords of the Arabs, a semitic tribe, as were the Hebrews. But the cement of faith was not enough to bind all the many peoples drawn to Islam. Arab unity, then as now, became more a name than a nation. Arab, which once meant one from Arabia, came to mean one who spoke Arabic and was a Moslem. Large chunks of the Arab empire broke off into semi-independence.

The Egyptians, the Seljuks, Crusaders, and finally the Ottoman Turks in the 16th century, took possession of the land once called Canaan (so named because of a rare purple dye pre-Israelite people used to color the robes of their leaders). But Canaan had been promised to Abraham, not the Frankish knight or the Seljuk, and they could not hold what they grasped and so became one with the shades of Cyrus and Sargon and Titus.

Yet, in the crowded ghettos of Europe, for all those thousands of years, the covenant

30

was remembered. "If I forget thee, O Jerusalem, let my right hand forget her cunning," began an ancient Hebrew prayer. And, in the middle of the last century, there were those who vowed the prayer would become more, that those cast like seed in alien lands of the world would once more grow in the land promised them.

In the 1860s there were only about 12,000 Jews in what is now Israel. For centuries they had lived as tradesmen and artisans. Much of the land had been innocent of a plow since bibilical times. But it was to this arid, stony earth that the Jews would return, inspired by their faith, driven by the pogroms of Russia and eastern Europe, and led by the words of their new prophets, the Zionists.

Zion had been the Jebusite name for Jerusalem. When David captured the city from them and brought the Ark that contained the covenant between Moses and Jehovah there, he made the name a symbol for his capital. In the 1880s Rabbi Samuel Mohilever organized the Lovers of Zion, a political committee organized to buy land in Palestine. Twenty years earlier, Moses Hess, who had married a Christian prostitute to show his defiance of Orthodox Jewry, had written a book called *Rome and Jerusalem* advocating a return by Jews to Palestine (the Roman name for the country).

But it was Theodor Herzl, a life-loving Viennese journalist, who also wrote bedroom comedy spiced with seductions and cuckolded husbands, who became the father of Zionism. He, as Paul, had had a vision. For Herzl it occurred when he was covering the trial of Captain Alfred Dreyfus, the French artillery officer framed in part because he was a Jew. At one time Herzl had considered being baptized. Then he heard French anti-Dreyfusard mobs calling "Death to the Jews!" Instead of baptism, he wrote a book, *Der Judenstaat*. It was a sensation among Jews. The wealthy scoffed. But the poor called him Herzl *ha-melech* (Herzl the King) and the first Zionist Congress at Basel, Switzerland, in 1897, declared its policy "to create for the Jewish people a homeland in Palestine secured by public law."

Old Jerusalem's Via Dolorosa, where Jesus carried His cross.

The Changing Face of Israel 1914-1956

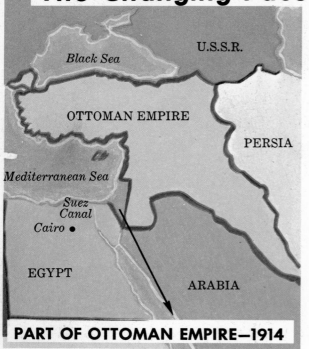

PART OF OTTOMAN EMPIRE—1914

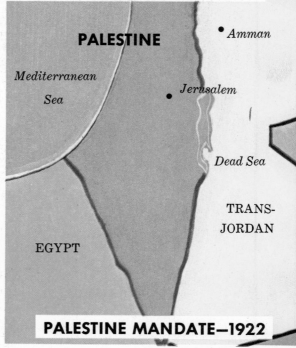

PALESTINE MANDATE—1922

There was one complication: The Turks ruled the land and the Arab landholders (effendis) owned it. The Turks scarcely would relinquish a part of their mortally ailing empire. But there were effendis who would sell if someone was insane enough to pay through the nose for their browned and thirsting land. A day would come when they would rue it, as Esau rued the day he traded Jacob his birthright for bread and pottage.

One of the principal buyers was Baron Edmond Rothschild, the Frenchman, who organized immigrant Jews on land he had purchased, built homes for them, and bought their produce for more than its worth to sustain the community. Several waves of immigrants came to Palestine in the last years of the century. The Arabs called them "children of death" because they worked in the malarial swamps and desert. In 1908 the first kibbutz was organized at Degania on the Sea of Galilee. Its communal life drew its inspiration from the Essenes, religious recluses, from Karl Marx, and from the short-lived Paris Commune of 1871.

The children of death flourished. By the end of World War I there were 100,000 Jews in Palestine. There were also about 600,000 Arabs, 100,000 of them nomads, the rest living under feudal bondage to the effendis.

Yet this barren land suddenly became a high card in the sly diplomatic dealing during the First World War. The purposes are obscure to this very day, but on November 2, 1917, the British Foreign Secretary, Lord Balfour, wrote a letter to Baron Rothschild. Some think it was done to appeal to the Jewish people of the United States to press the American war effort, or to secure Suez. Lloyd George, then Prime Minister of Britain, was to say later that it was done for "propagandistic purposes." In any event, Balfour wrote:

"His Majesty's Government view with favor the establishment in Palestine of a national home for the Jewish people and will use their best endeavors to facilitate

32

U.N. PARTITION PLAN—1947

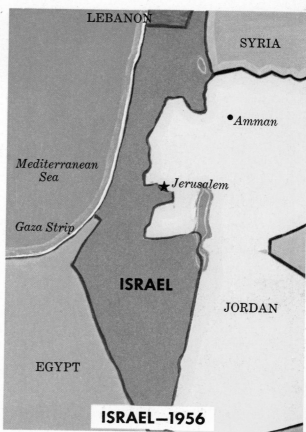

ISRAEL—1956

the achievement of this object, it being clearly understood that nothing shall be done which may prejudice the civil and existing rights of existing non-Jewish elements in Palestine. . . ."

For the Jews, it came as a new covenant, a promise from Downing Street to match that from Mount Sinai. For the Arabs, it was a brutal betrayal. For 1,500 years, they, not the Jews, had held the land. And for two years before the Balfour Declaration, they had held something else. For in 1915 the British Commissioner in Egypt, Sir Arthur Henry McMahon, had written the Grand Sherif of Mecca promising the Arabs certain Middle Eastern territories if they would revolt against the Turks. Palestine was not mentioned by name.

Nonetheless, the Arabs, led by T. E. Lawrence—Lawrence of Arabia—did revolt. The British, under Allenby, routed the Turks. The Ottoman Empire collapsed. And Britain, having twice promised, had sparked a fire kindled when Ishmael and Isaac, brothers, had gone their separate ways.

Maybe it is because they are so close that Arab and Jew fight so bitterly. And close they are. The Jew greets: *sholom aleichem*—peace. The Arab greets: *salaam alaykum*—peace. The Jewish declaration of faith, the Shema, says, "Hear O Israel, the Lord our God, the Lord is One." The Arab prays, *La illaha illa Allah*—"There is no god but God."

There is nothing so bitter as a family feud, lest it be strife over religion. The Arabs and Jews have both. Once, in Sinai, Moses drew water from a rock. But when the British Mandate over Palestine began in 1922 there were to be no miracles. There was to be no Solomon, only a nation, weakened by its own war, muddling through as best it could and not always that. The peacemaker was not blessed either of Isaac or Ishmael.

The Arabs of Palestine in 1922 were poor, dominated by their feudal lords, the effendis, who also saw rising Arabic nationalism as a threat to their tenure of the land. Perhaps these courteous aristocrats who lived by tradition lay closer to the heart of the English-man than the polyglot, ambitious Jews. These Arabs wanted the status quo. So did the British—peace in the land so close to the Suez artery to their empire. The Jews wanted peace, too. But they also wanted the land.

A census of that time, 1922, counted the Jews as 12.9 percent of the population. But to the Jews their ancient words of farewell, "Next year in Jerusalem," had become reality. In 1925 alone, 33,800 of them immigrated to their Promised Land. In 1929 the Jewish population stood at 18.9 percent. And yet the effendi kept selling his birthright. Poor land, hardly fit for goats. Yet the Jew made it flower. He developed Tel Aviv into a growing city. The Jewish Agency, a shadow government, built schools, hospitals and kibbutzim in Sharon and Galilee and the Jezreel Valley. Jews abroad raised money for land purchase through the Jewish Na-

tional Fund. In 1914 the Jews held title to 177 square miles in Palestine. In 1935 they owned 500 square miles. In 1922 the British Colonial Secretary said Britain did not contemplate "the disappearance or the subordination of the Arab population, language or culture in Palestine." For once Winston Churchill misread history.

By purchase and energy and immigration a 20th-century people were taking over a medieval wilderness. By 1935 the Jews had spent a million and a half dollars draining malarial marshland. The Arabs had spent nothing. By 1948 the National Fund had founded 233 villages, settled 83,000 Jews, and planted five million trees. The result was inevitable.

In 1929 the Arabs rioted. They raided Hebron, killing 60 Jews. This brought a White Paper from London which established closer control over Jewish immigration and protec-

An Israeli truck is shot up by sniper fire and the driver slain by Arabs at Jerusalem: 1948.

tion for Arab landholders. The Jews called it a Black Paper. It settled nothing. Both sides took to arms.

In the early days the Arabs had raided the kibbutzim, generally on a Sabbath, with cudgels and knives. The Jews, in turn, maintained their own watchmen, the *shomrim*, who patrolled at night much as the hired gunmen of the American West. It was not enough. A Russian, Vladimir Jabotinsky, who had been a newspaperman, a mule skinner and an officer with Allenby, now became the first Jewish warrior leader since Bar Kochba. His army was called Z'va Haganah—Army of Defense. It was illegal under the mandate, but the British tolerated it because it saved them the expense of garrisoning their own men. A British captain, Orde Wingate, who was to become a hero in Burma in World War II, organized the Jews into Special Night Squads, guerillas who fought the Arab by dark. Wingate's widow was later to drop the bible of this Lawrence of the Hebrews from a plane over a Jewish community besieged during the 1948 war.

For some Jews the self-defense Haganah was not enough. Some students of Hebrew University organized the Irgun, a terrorist group. The Haganah issued a critical pamphlet saying "Thou shall not kill." The Irgun clandestine radio replied: "An eye for an eye and a tooth for a tooth." The Irgun had its own code of honor. Its "soldiers" always wore identifying armbands when they attacked. They always gave advance warning. In 1946, when terrorists blew up the King David Hotel in Jerusalem, killing 91 persons, they telephoned a warning 25 minutes before.

The Arabs, meanwhile, led by the violently anti-semitic Grand Mufti of Jerusalem, had demanded the British stop all immigration and land sales to Jews. When the British refused, the Arabs revolted and bands of mercenaries, mostly from Syria, raided the Jewish communities.

The British sent a commission to Palestine in 1937 which recommended Palestine be partitioned. The fighting merely intensified. In 1939, the British issued another White Paper. It declared that a Jewish state in Palestine was contrary to Britain's obligations to the Arabs and promised independence of the mandated land within 10 years, with Arab and Jew sharing authority. Immigration was to be limited to 75,000 for the next five years and determined thereafter with Arab approval. Jewish land purchase was restricted in 95 percent of the country.

The Jewish reaction would have been violent at any time. But in 1939 Adolf Hitler had been in power six years. In April of that year three ships bearing refugees from Germany and Rumania arrived in Palestine. The British refused to let them land. Colonial Secretary Malcolm MacDonald said they must return whence they came.

"Does that mean to concentration camps?" asked Philip Noel-Baker in Parliament.

"The responsibility rests with those responsible for organizing illegal importation," replied the Secretary.

The Jewish Agency asked for the immediate admission of 20,000 Polish children and 10,000 Balkan men. The British said no. They went to Maidanek and Auschwitz instead.

In 1940 a terrorist plot misfired and 260 refugees who had been denied permission to land were killed on the ship *Patria* in Haifa harbor. A boy of 14, Eliyahu Ben Hakim, witnessed the explosion. Four years later he assassinated Lord Moyne, Britain's minister in Cairo.

As the world slowly learned that a new Nebuchadnezzar was burning the Jews, the pressures on Britain, which wanted the allegiance of the newly independent Arab states in her battle for survival, became extreme. The British Labor Party spoke for more than itself at its 1944 party conference when it declared:

"There is surely neither hope nor meaning in a 'Jewish national home' unless we are prepared to let the Jews, if they wish, enter this tiny land in such numbers as to become a majority. There was a strong case before the war. There is an irresistible one now, after the unspeakable atrocities of the German Nazi plan to kill all the Jews in Europe."

Holy Jerusalem lighted by the hell fire of war: 1948.

1956: The devastation in Port Said.

But those not in power can only pledge, not guarantee. When Labor became the government in 1945, the pledge was not honored. To Britain, Arab tranquility over Suez and Arabian oil were manna and water for her war-weakened people. The Jews asked immediate immigration of 100,000 survivors of Hitler's ovens. Britain continued the 1,500-a-month immigration policy of the '39 White Paper, a document Churchill had called a "base betrayal." But Churchill was no longer prime minister.

The Jews came anyway.

They came on an old paddle steamer called the *Atlantic* as typhus raged through the ship. They came, 350 of them, on a 75-foot sailboat and 231 of them drowned in a storm. They tried to come on the 180-foot cattleboat *Sturma* but it capsized and of its 769 passengers, but one survived.

Posters appeared in Palestine declaring the British High Commissioner of Palestine was "wanted for the murder by drowning of 800 refugees on board the *Sturma.*"

Two British sergeants were hanged in an orchard and their bodies booby-trapped. Drunken British soldiers fired at Jews. In Tel Aviv, British troops separated the Jews by dyeing their foreheads and shouted "Heil Hitler" in mockery. A schoolboy was flogged for carrying pamphlets.

Young Jews of the Stern Gang bombed British police barracks and teen-agers learned how to fire machine guns from a manual of arms written in ancient Hebraic. Herzl, the Zionist, had once asked, "Why, who of us knows enough Hebrew to even buy a railroad ticket?" Now the tongue of the prophets had new words, for "tommy gun" and "clip" and "bullet."

The group's founder, Abraham Stern, shot by the British during the war "while trying to escape," was a poet who took the code name "Yair"—from the ancient leader of the Jews at Masada who had committed mass suicide rather than surrender to Rome. Before his death, Stern wrote an anthem for the Underground:

Fight your way home, eternal tramp,
Your house we shall rejoin and mend the broken lamp.

An earlier war; a younger Dayan.

The Jews, "swept by the wind to land that was not theirs," fought their way home.

Two sailing ships reached Haifa in 1946. The British brought up a division by land and two cruisers. The refugees dived into the sea and began swimming to their Promised Land. British sailors had to knock them unconscious to drag them from the water. Sixty thousand Jews, led by survivors of Belsen and Buchenwald clad in their prison uniforms, marched in protest of British internment of refugees on Cyprus and the Mauritius. The Haganah, no longer just a self-defense force, blew up 100 bridges and railroad tracks the night of October 31, 1945.

Two weeks later, Ernest Bevin, the British Foreign Secretary, announced creation of a joint Anglo-American committee to decide the future of Palestine. He cautioned the Jews not "to push to the head of the queue" and turned down an American request to permit 100,000 refugees to immigrate. The old rate would continue, he said, depending on "the generosity of our Arab friends."

A year later, Bevin told a Labor conference the Americans were sending Jews to Palestine "because they don't want them in New York."

On April 20, 1947, the Anglo-American commission recommended immigration of the 100,000 refugees. It said nothing of partition. Bevin, that same year, agreed to immigration of 96,000 refugees over a two-year period. After that, the UN would decide the land's future with ultimately a Jewish minority under an Arab majority. The Jews turned the plan down.

Ten days later, the British turned the whole matter over to the UN. Solomon had had enough.

The UN announced a partition plan in August, 1947. The Jews accepted it. The Arabs did not. Egypt, Jordan, Syria, Iraq, Saudi Arabia and Yemen vowed a war of extermination. The UN voted partition in November, 1947, by 33–13 with the help of behind-the-scenes diplomacy by Andrei Gromyko, Russia's UN delegate. Britain, which said it would not vote for a plan not acceptable to both sides, announced it would surrender its mandate May 15, 1948.

After the UN vote, which both the United States and Russia supported, Jews sang in the streets of New York and Tel Aviv and in the DP camps. But in Palestine, it was civil war. Arabs, who before the British turned back Rommel at El Alemein had marked the houses of Jews they would take when the Nazis came, attacked Jewish convoys carrying food to Jerusalem. The British refused to allow armored cars to escort the convoys "because it arouses the Arabs." Seventy-seven Jews, on their way to the Hadassah Hospital and Hebrew University on Mount Scopus, were killed in an Arab attack.

At the Arab village of Deir Yassin, near Jerusalem, the Stern and Irgun terrorists attacked a settlement of peaceful Arabs. A total of 251 Arabs, including women and children, were brutally murdered. Moderate Jews were appalled. David Ben-Gurion, the Jewish leader, personally phoned King Abdullah of Jordan to apologize. But there was no longer time for apologies. Arabs fled en masse—70,000 from Haifa alone, despite Jewish pleas that they stay.

On April 1, 1948, the Jews launched Operation Nachson against the Arabs, a coordinated attack armed with automatic weapons that arrived at the last moment.

(Nachson was the first Jew to jump into the Red Sea during the Exodus.)

True to their word, the British pulled out on schedule. And, as the last British soldiers left on May 14, 1948, Ben-Gurion rose at a special session of the Jewish National Council in the Museum of Modern Art in Tel Aviv and declared the independence of the state of Israel "on this Sabbath eve, the fifth day of Iyar in the year 5708." The Jews had come home.

The army of this new Zion began hostilities with barely 10,000 rifles, many of them stolen from the British during the war. They had a few armored cars from the Jewish Settlement Police of the mandate. The Haganah numbered about 20,000 with an equal number of home guards. But by Operation Black, so called because it occurred at night, the Jews airlifted weapons from Czechoslovakia, the same country whose sale of arms to Egypt in 1955 was a key factor in the 1956 war.

The UN mediator, Count Folke Bernadotte, won a cease-fire June 11, 1948, but fighting broke out for 10 days July 9 and again in October, by which time Bernadotte had been murdered, probably by Stern terrorists. The Israelis won the Negev, where Ishmael had lived, and Galilee, by the time an armistice was signed. The Arabs, humiliated, signed but never put the armistice into effect, declaring they were at war until Israel was exterminated. Under the armistice Israel added 2,380 square miles to the 5,760 square miles granted by partition.

The Arab nations placed an embargo on goods to Israel, eventually closing the Suez Canal to any such shipments. Yet Israel, aided by a total of $2 billion from overseas Jewry and $822 million in restitution from West Germany, prospered.

And as she prospered, so did the 700,000 Arabs who had fled their homeland suffer. Israel offered to take some back and to pay for resettlement of others. But President Nasser of Egypt refused to let the refugees leave their camps in the Gaza Strip. Lebanon, precariously balanced between its Christian and Moslem population, did not want more Arabs in her land to tip the scales. Iraq had a surplus of land and a shortage of labor, but no effort was made to move the refugees there. Only Jordan gave them full civil rights. But Jordan was a poor country at best, and Israel had taken some of her best land in the war. So the refugees lived their years in the camps, fed not by their fellow Arabs but by the United Nations Relief and Works Agency, 70 percent of whose budget came from the United States.

In Israel, 150,000 Arabs had stayed behind. Except in border areas they received full rights of citizenship. Seven Arabs now sit in the Knesset, the Jewish parliament. The Arabs have their own radio station. Their living standard has become as high as any in the Arab world. Bedouin agriculture in the Negev has increased fivefold; the Arab mortality rate dropped two-thirds; the Arab life expectancy increased from 48 in 1948 to 73 in 1966.

But in the Arab world, many lived but for one thing: the death of the Israeli state.

Despite UN mixed armistice commissions, Arab raiders crossed regularly into Israel to kill and destroy. In 1953 Egypt blockaded the Straits of Tiran and two years later forbade Israeli commercial flights over the Gulf of Aqaba. In 1955 the Czechs sold Nasser 200 modern planes and 230 tanks. In October, 1955, Syria and Egypt formed a joint military command which Jordan joined a year later. Just as the Palestinian refugees sneaked across the border to steal food from fields that had once been theirs, so would the Arabs take their land from the infidel who heeded not the word of Mohammed.

But, ringed by the scimitar of Islam, the Jews were not alone. Britain, a weary lion whose empire was gone as the Ottoman's, had been roused to anger when Nasser nationalized the Suez Canal in 1956. Joined with France, the British planned to seize the Canal and told Israel so.

The Jews called it Operation Kadesh, after the place in the wilderness where the people of Israel tarried on the way to the Promised Land. The operation lasted seven days and Israeli forces, under General Moshe Dayan, overran the Sinai Peninsula, killing 3,000 Egyptians. The other Arab nations stayed within their borders while their brother Arabs died.

There was no initial air strike at Egyptian air bases in 1956. Dayan wanted to disguise the full impact of the Israeli march as long as possible, to deceive the Egyptians into thinking it was just a large-scale raid, not a general war. Israeli paratroops took the heights of the Mitla Pass near the Canal, and motorized columns bypassed Egyptian strongholds along the coast to reach the Canal with maximum speed.

The Egyptians fled at the approach of the Israelis. In El Arish, for instance, Jewish soldiers entered a hospital that had been left with its sick and wounded by the doctors and nurses. An Egyptian soldier on the operating table had been left midway during an amputation of his leg. He bled to death.

Under powerful diplomatic pressure in the UN, Israel withdrew from Sinai and the Anglo-French forces from the Canal. A UN Emergency Force moved into the Gaza Strip and into Sharm el Sheikh at the mouth of the Gulf of Aqaba. Nasser agreed to the stationing of the UN troops—providing they would be withdrawn at his request. Israel, arguing that such a condition made the force meaningless, refused to have the UN soldiers stationed on its territory.

As ardently as had the Zionists, the Arabs still thirsted for what had been theirs. In July, 1965, Nasser, for instance, declared: "The war between us and Israel is inevitable."

Ben-Gurion seemed to agree. "If they educate—I don't think that is the right word —their people to a belief that Israel is a cancer that must be wiped out, they inevitably become victims of their own propaganda."

Propaganda or not, the Arabs took steps. Russia, which had recognized the Israeli state two days after it was declared independent, sent modern jets and tanks and missiles to Egypt and Syria.

In January, 1964, an Arab High Command was organized and later that year the Arab states voted to collect $43 million a year to arm Syria, Jordan and Lebanon for the single purpose of fighting Israel. One-third of the money was to come from the oil-rich sheikdom of Kuwait, whose vast deposits in Britain were a pillar of the pound sterling.

But all was not unity in the tent of the Arab. Jordan refused to have the newly organized Palestine Liberation Army, made up of refugees, within its borders, fearing a takeover by Nasser, who had implied publicly that Jordan's King Hussein ought to be assassinated. In Yemen, Egyptian troops fought to support the government against the deposed ruler who was backed by Saudi Arabia. In Tunisia, President Bourguiba called on the Arab states to replace military with political pressure against Israel. Faisal, King of Saudi Arabia, talked of an Islamic Alliance with the Shah of Iran. And in 1961, Iraq threatened to take over Kuwait.

The Western powers tried to ride two camels at once, hoping to placate the Arabian oil states while trying to atone to Israel for the Nazi massacres of the Jews. The United States sent large shipments of food to Nasser who spent the money thus saved him on Russian arms. The U.S., meanwhile, was clandestinely shipping arms to Israel via West Germany.

In Israel, the Jews, now numbering 2.5 million, armed for the future. And worked for it. In 1948 Israel's agricultural production was worth $15 million. In 1966 the figure was $400 million. In the same time Egyptian farm output increased 22 percent.

The Jews, whose ashes once fertilized German Victory Gardens, symbolically planted 6 million trees in the Valley of Martyrs in honor of the Nazi victims.

Oil, Auschwitz, Zion, Suez, Arab unity and Arab disunity: all words in a question: whose is the land? Is it of the Jews, one of the most ancient of peoples, who can say, as few if any others can, that they won independence in the year 5708 of their history, say it in the land their God promised them? Or does Esau retain his birthright, even though he sold some of it and had the rest taken from him, as Babylon took it from

Assyria, as Moslem took it from Byzantine, as Ottoman took it from Egyptian?

Is it given man the wisdom to have scales to balance such things?

The children of Abraham, in any case, would not wait, neither of them. In November of 1966, Israelis raided along the Syrian border. The Jews said it was in retaliation for Syrian raids. Forty houses were destroyed in a Jordanian village by Israelis. At the UN, the big powers grumbled. On April 6, 1967, it is said that a Syrian jet swept low over Israeli fields. Israeli jets shot down six Syrian fighters.

Nasser, his Yemeni campaign an embarrassing stalemate, his United Arab Federation with Syria a failure, apparently saw a chance. It was a chance to regain his lost stature in the eyes of the Arabs. And it was a chance to drive the infidel into the sea.

Syria and Egypt mobilized. So did Israel.

Then, at 10 o'clock on the evening of May 16, Major General Indar Jit Rikhye, commander of the 3,400-man UN Emergency Force, received a message. It was from General Mohammed Fawzy, chief of staff of the Egyptian army. It asked withdrawal "of all UN troops which install OPs [observation posts] along our borders."

The message was rushed to UN Secretary-General U Thant. He received it as he was dressing for dinner. The next day the UN troops reported that Egyptian soldiers and armor were moving up to the border. At 6:30 A.M. the UN commander said Egyptian troops had occupied an OP at El Sabha and had advanced past UN camps at El Quseima and El Sabha toward the border.

On May 18, at 7 P.M., Thant handed a message to the permanent Egyptian delegate to the UN, Mohamed Awad el Kony, to be delivered to the Egyptian Minister for Foreign Affairs, Mahmoud Riad:

"I am proceeding to issue instructions for the necessary arrangements to be put in train without delay for the orderly withdrawal of the force . . ."

The peacemaker who had stood between Isaac and Ishmael stood there no more.

Trenches and shattered walls are the scars of past wars at Jerusalem's Mandelbaum Gate.

JIHAD!

It was high noon in Cairo, May 16, and most people were thinking of lunch and the customary three-hour siesta to follow. At first no one paid notice to the traffic jam in Tahrir Square, the broad esplanade in the center of the Egyptian capital. Funerals in a nearby mosque were always tieing up traffic in Tahrir Square. But this was no funeral.

The first dun-colored half-track nosed into view on the two-lane corniche bordering the Nile. Then another. Then a Russian-built truck packed with soldiers in camouflaged battle dress. Then Russian-built tanks. Armored personnel - carriers. Jeeps. Trucks pulling 40-millimeter antitank guns. For three hours they came.

They could have used a superhighway that bypassed Tahrir Square. Instead the convoy moved through Garden City, one of Cairo's most fashionable residential districts, in full view of the foreign embassies.

A few Egyptians stood on the sidewalks and cheered. Most just looked on, wondering what it was all about. Plainly, President Nasser was moving troops. But where?

And this note General Rikhye received a few hours later at his command post in the Gaza Strip far to the north asking removal of the UN troops: what was behind that?

Rikhye told the smartly-dressed Egyptian brigadier who had brought the message from General Fawzy that he would have to refer the matter to UN headquarters in New York. He did. Thant replied: "Be firm in maintaining UNEF [United Nations Emergency Force] position while being as understanding and diplomatic as possible in your relations with U.A.R. officials."

For his part Thant sought an urgent meeting with Cairo's permanent UN representative, Ambassador el Kony, for clarification. He also told Cairo that any request for withdrawal of the UN forces must come directly to the Secretary-General from the Egyptian government.

If anyone needed any clarification of what was going on, the official Cairo paper *Al Ahram,* edited by Mohammad Hassanein Heikal, an old crony of Nasser's, supplied it next morning.

"Our troops move to confront the Zionist enemy," cried the headlines. "More than 80,000 elite Egyptian units move to the Sinai front."

At 6 A.M. Cairo Radio broadcast an alert to all Egyptian troops:

"The state of preparedness of the Egyptian Army will increase to the full level of preparedness for war, beginning 1430 hours last Sunday [May 14]. The armed forces are to be in full preparedness to carry out any combat tasks on the Israel front in accordance with developments."

Was this bluff? Or was it war? Gamal Abdel Nasser had long since proved himself able in both. He had fought heroically in the 1948 war against Israel. And he had long posed himself as the leader of a unified Arab world, a world which in fact was neither unified nor which he led. But he

Support for Nasser in Beirut.

43

was its dominant personality. If Nasser was calling for a *jihad,* a holy war, against Israel, any Arab ruler held back at his peril.

On May 18 Nasser demanded that all 3,400 UN soldiers—Brazilians, Canadians, Danes, Norwegians, Swedes and Yugoslavians—leave the Gaza Strip and Sinai "for their own protection." Thant, believing the troops were there only with Egyptian permission, agreed to order them out.

There would be those who would say Thant should have delayed any abrupt action by technical evasions. They would call the blitz to come "Thant's War." One diplomat said the Secretary-General "doesn't seem to understand how to delay a crisis like this." Israel's Foreign Minister, Abba Eban, said the decision to withdraw was "disastrously swift." It may even have caught Nasser by surprise. But it was done. Syria had long taunted Nasser for hiding behind the "glass shield" of the UN. Now it was gone. Israeli and Egyptian soldiers watched across the border as the UN troops struck their blue and white colors.

"War is inevitable," said Heikal's paper. Posters went up depicting an Egyptian strangling a Jew who was trying to hide behind an evil-looking Uncle Sam. Just after midnight on May 19 Sawt al Arab— the Voice of Arabs—broadcast an Order of the Day from the Egyptian commander in Sinai, Abdul Mohsen Mortagi:

"Egyptian forces have taken up positions in accordance with a definite plan. Our forces are definitely ready to carry the battle beyond the borders of Egypt."

So they seemed.

The Egyptian government flew a group of Western correspondents up into Sinai to show the armed array. At El Arish, Russian-made MIG-21 fighters gleamed in the sunlight behind revetments at the big jet fighter strip. Tanks rolled past, their crews trim and alert.

"It was impressive," wrote one of the newsmen, Garven Hudgins of the Associated Press, "and the impression grew that this time things would be different in the Sinai if the Israelis attacked."

The commander of the El Arish sector, Major General Saad Shazly, a charming 45-year-old officer who had trained at Fort Benning, entertained the reporters at a luncheon on a terrace overlooking the Mediterranean. He reminisced of his days as a paratrooper in the 1956 war, and talked of Western newsmen ("Weren't they all government agents?") and of the U.S. position on the Middle East crisis ("It was unfair").

In the distance, heavy artillery boomed practice rounds.

In Gaza, truckloads of ragged Palestine Liberation Army troops, refugees who had been clamoring for 19 years to return to their homeland, passed by cheering onlookers. The Egyptians were handing out 30-caliber rifles from Red China to all comers. They explained to the instant soldiers how to fire machine guns.

"We are going back to our land. We are ready to die for our land! Death to Johnson!" they cried, conveniently in English.

The barracks of the former Swedish UN troops was deserted. Beer cans, painted white, that had once spelled out the number of the unit, had been rearranged. Now they spelled in Arabic: "Return to Palestine."

On May 22 Nasser made a move that was far closer to war than bluff. He announced a blockade of the Gulf of Aqaba, Israel's sea lane to Africa and Asia. Israel had said in the past such a move would mean war. In 1956 it had.

Even as Nasser spoke, Thant was flying to Cairo to talk peace. "When U Thant flew in," an Egyptian businessman recalled, "we saw his grim face and we saw the confident face of our president. That reflected our confident feelings, too. We read reports of how Gamal had assured U Thant that Egypt did not intend to attack Israel but was only asserting its rights to territorial regions which Israel had illegally acquired in her brazen attack in 1956. We also had news of how the Americans, who we know are staunch supporters of Israel, were calling on the Israelis to avoid starting a war."

The newly arrived U.S. ambassador to Cairo, Richard Nolte, a 47-year-old scholar

Egyptians enthusiastically support Nasser's war call at the Gaza Strip.

who spoke Arabic but had no diplomatic experience, said "I am not one of those who subscribe to the view that there is now a Middle East crisis." Two days later, however, he told newsmen he thought the situation was "dicey."

But as the days passed after the blockade announcement, some of the pressure seemed to ease. Nasser held a press conference on May 28, his first since the Suez crisis of 11 years before. He reasserted Egypt's claims to the Strait of Tiran, only three miles wide, at the mouth of the Gulf of Aqaba. The Strait was well within their territorial 12-mile limit, the Egyptians claimed, although maritime law said that when several countries shared a seaway, it was considered international waters. But

Nasser struck a note of caution. Israel would be destroyed, he said, but he would be patient. "I can wait a year or 10 years."

Also for the first time in years, he acknowledged that the United States had played a role in halting the 1956 fighting. Previously he had given sole credit to the Russians.

The next day he talked 90 minutes with an ambassador from another Arab nation. "Nasser is sure there will be no war. He is convinced he has won," the ambassador reported.

But Nasser had called for a *jihad* against the infidel. The Jews had long lived with that. But he had also sealed a lifeline without which they could not live, not for long. In Jerusalem and Tel Aviv, public transport became chaotic. The bus drivers, the ticket

45

Israeli troops march eastward in the Judean hills.

takers, weren't around to keep the lines working. They had been called up to drive other machines, machines of war.

Reservists all over the country lined up at improvised registration centers. Many elderly men exempt from duty joined the queues. Air raid shelter signs were newly plastered to ancient walls. Housewives placed blackout tape on windows and lined up at blood banks. In the kibbutzim, children dug slit trenches. Police in the Negev closely eyed the tents of the Bedouins. People in the narrow waist of Israel could see Jordanian tanks in the fields where Christ had walked. Arab shepherds, in their ancient dress, carried submachine guns slung from their shoulders. Camouflage netting went over the black and brown tents of the nomads to conceal the artillery beneath. Jordan's capital of Amman was blacked out. Even cigarettes were forbidden.

Whoever had started it, it had started.

On May 29 Soviet Premier Alexei Kosygin sent Nasser what amounted to a Soviet guarantee of the Egyptian blockade. It was, Nasser said, "just the stand we have been waiting for." He did not elaborate on the details but said Moscow had furnished "all sorts of arms we wanted" in the past. "Allah will certainly help us to restore the status quo as of before 1948."

And it appeared Allah would have the help of Ivan.

What the U.S. would do was not clear. *Again!* The United States in the UN supported Thant's appeal for a cooling-off period to permit a diplomatic search for a solution. The State Department contended that the Gulf of Aqaba should be open to all nations. Nasser replied that Egypt would consider such a declaration by the maritime powers "an act of aggression against our sovereignty and a prelude to military action." Britain was cool to any proposed demonstration to force the blockade. France's President Charles De Gaulle, enjoying good relations with both sides, refused to commit himself either way.

The American Sixth Fleet slipped its cables and left port for a rendezvous off Crete. There, the carriers *Saratoga* and

America, with two missile-firing cruisers, 15 destroyers and a number of submarines and support craft, as well as 2,000 marines, waited. A Russian fleet of 10 ships headed through the Dardanelles from the Black Sea while Russian trawlers monitored the American fleet, watching the low gray shapes spread along the horizon. Once before, in 1958, the fleet had landed marines in Lebanon when communists seemed about to take over the government. But there had not been Viet Nam then. The U.S. could fight but was clearly reluctant to do so. One war was enough.

Nasser himself breathed hot and cold. Egypt would not call on the Soviet Union for help if America intervened, he said, but "would leave that to the friendly powers themselves to decide." But in Syria, Nureddin el Atassi, the Chief of State, said his country was "ready to start the final battle of liberation." Saudi Arabia, whose troops had been fighting Egypt's in Yemen, announced general mobilization "in fulfillment of the kingdom's avowed policy on the Palestine question." King Faisal, whatever his sympathies, had no choice but to join the *jihad.* To do otherwise would risk his overthrow.

Yet it was a strange array that girded against Israel. Not only had Saudi Arabia been in undeclared battle with Egypt, Faisal's deposed brother, ex-King Saud, had received sumptuous sanctuary in Cairo where he sniped at his brother's policies. Syria delighted in calling Faisal names, one of the less insulting that of "the bearded bigot." When a mine blew up at the Syrian-Jordanian border during the crisis, King Hussein ordered the border closed and expelled the Syrian ambassador. To the Syrians, Hussein was the "Hashemite harlot" who collaborated with U.S. imperialism. Nasser had called Hussein and Faisal "traitors who plot against us in the name of our religion." Ahmed Shukairy, head of the ragtag Palestine Liberation Army whose goal was a Palestine Republic, had said only a year ago that "Liberation of Palestine should start with liberation of Jordan from its reactionary, treacherous regime."

Jordan, whose borders had little rhyme

Jordanian recoiless rifle unit zeros in on Israeli sector of Jerusalem.

Gamal Abdel Nasser and U Thant confer in Cairo.

or reason, had been conjured out of the wastes of the deserts after World War I with British backing. It was repayment to the Hashemite tribal Sheik Abdullah, who, with Lawrence of Arabia, had fought out of the Arabian desert against the Ottomans. Jordan's Arab neighbors could never forgive her for "selling out" to the British. Or so they said.

But the shifting sands of Arab unity underwent all but an earthquake May 30 when Hussein flew his own Caravelle jet to Cairo to embrace Nasser, who three weeks before had called him a traitor and agent of the Central Intelligence Agency. The two signed a defense pact and Nasser emotionally called Hussein "brother." To complete the portrait of family fealty, Shukairy sat beaming by Hussein's side. Then he flew back with him to Jordan. If Hussein had not brought peace closer with the Israelis, he had with the passionate followers of Shukairy among the Palestinian refugees in Jordan. And perhaps that, at the moment, was more important to his throne.

Nasser had reason to feel patriarchal. He had brought the children of Arabia together under his banner. He had twice gambled and won—getting rid of the UN and blockading Aqaba. And Israeli Prime Minister Levi Eshkol said his nation would continue to work with the big powers to try and seek a reopening of the Gulf. This suggested that Israel wanted to negotiate, not

fight, her way out of Aqaba. In international law a blockade was an act of war. Egypt had blockaded. And there was no war. Nasser had crossed over into Sinai. But Sinai wasn't the Rubicon. Or so it seemed.

It did not seem quite so certain the day after Hussein left—May 31. The Israelis announced that Moshe Dayan had been named Defense Minister.

Dayan had been the Gideon of his people in the 1956 campaign, its designer, its leader. Did his return to power mean a return to the Sinai?

Dayan had become increasingly active in the Rafi Party of David Ben-Gurion, the Israeli hero of 1948. As Prime Minister, Eshkol traditionally held the defense ministry. But many of his people seemed to think he was irresolute, that he was waiting too long while the Egyptian garrote across the Straits of Tiran grew tighter. Israel did not have the resources for a long campaign or blockade. She must either fight a swift war or die a long death. With the appointment of Dayan, there was strong evidence that she had chosen.

"May 31 is the fateful day," said an Egyptian close to the government. "Our papers make it clear the Israelis have brought in a war cabinet, meant to fight our army. High up among Nasser's close advisers, they know that there will be a war. And they know they are not prepared for it."

50

On paper they were. Or so it seemed. The authoritative British Institute for Strategic Studies put the relative strength of the armies this way:

Israel: 60,000 regulars, 204,000 reservists, about 800 tanks of U.S. and British manufacture, about 250 self-propelled guns, missiles, about 350 planes, mostly French.

Egypt: 190,000 regulars of whom 50,000 were in Yemen, 120,000 reservists, about 1,200 tanks, mostly Russian, more than 550 planes, mostly Soviet.

Syria: 60,000 regulars, 50,000 reservists, about 600 tanks, mostly Russian, and at least 100 Russian planes.

Jordan: 35,000 regulars, 35,000 reservists, about 132 tanks and 12 combat planes.

Iraq sent men to Jordan in support roles. Other Arab countries, such as Algeria with its Russian jets, stood ready if called.

Yet the Arab world seemed strangely unwarlike. In Cairo, workers listlessly piled sandbags in front of government buildings. Cairo's International Airport seemed virtually undefended. Streets in Damascus were lined with "Death to Israel" posters but there was little tension in the bazaars. Or so it seemed. In the garden of the Damascus Officers Club, officers passed the evenings sipping glasses of tea and smoking water pipes. The well-to-do danced rock 'n' roll at discotheques and the less affluent crowded cabarets to watch the belly dancers.

In Israel the streets were empty. The young were gone. Those left behind sat by their radios, in silence, as though awaiting a new Angel of Death on a new Passover Eve. Perhaps they heard Nasser's words over Cairo Radio, for he was speaking to them, the Jews of Israel:

"We face you in battle and are burning with desire to start in order to obtain revenge. This will make the world realize what the Arabs are and what the Jews are."

South of Suez, the U.S. aircraft carrier *Intrepid* slid slowly into the Red Sea and Egyptians hooted at it from the shore. The Pentagon denied she was heading for Aqaba. The *Intrepid* was a man-of-war and the war was in Viet Nam, not Aqaba. Or so it seemed.

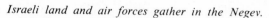

Israeli land and air forces gather in the Negev.

Israeli half-tracks cut across the desert toward El Arish.

MONDAY

"... SCATTER HIM IN THE WILDERNESS ..."

■ Across the bitter wastes and the few flowering valleys of the Middle East, across the years and the centuries of great wars and small border raids without number, who can say when one war begins and one war ends?

Who can say if the first blow was a pre-dawn Egyptian mortar attack that set the wheat fields of a kibbutz afire, wrecked cow-sheds, killed livestock? Who can say if the war began with jet planes propelled by the ghetto fear of a new nation surrounded by hostile camps, or with the angry harangue of a dictator, or with the seething humiliation of an Arab refugee?

On the morning of June 5, 1967, the sun burned its way through the early haze rising from the Negev and Sinai deserts. Egyptian troops were arrayed in two main lines across the harsh sands. On the other side, Israeli forces were also poised in full alert, Now, suddenly, there was no room between them for reason or restraint.

At more than two dozen military fields, west in Egypt, north in Syria and Iraq and east in Jordan, Arab air power lay at rest, planes parked in revetments and in neat military rows along the open black strips in the deserts and on the plateaus. Few planes were in the air.

But in Israel, where pilots sleep next to their planes even in times of relative peace, aircraft patrolled the skies from Haifa in the north to Eilat, the picturesque southern port at the Gulf of Aqaba.

At 8 A.M. Israeli time, a message flashed to Israeli airfields:

"Battle Order of the Officer Commanding, Israeli Air Force. Urgent. To All Units:

"Soldiers of the Air Force, the blustering and swashbuckling Egyptian Army is moving against us to annihilate our people ...

"Fly on, attack the enemy, pursue him to ruination, draw his fangs, scatter him in the wilderness, so that the people of Israel may live in peace in our land, and the future generations be secured."

Pilots sprinted to their waiting planes, French-built Mirages, Mystères, Super Mystères. The airfields around Tel Aviv screamed with the anger of jet engines. Planes in the air were directed to prearranged targets.

The Israeli strategy was to strike quickly with surprise. Catch the enemy planes on the ground. Baffle and elude their radar. And so, throughout the morning, wave after wave of the needle-nosed attack planes roared off to pummel enemy airfields and radar bases in Syria, Jordan, Iraq and Egypt—especially Egypt. For Egypt, there was a special plan to avoid detection.

Israeli jets flew almost due west from Tel Aviv out over the Mediterranean glinting in the morning sun. They flew low in flights of threes and fours—barely 500 feet off the water—to keep the high Judean hills between them and the eye of Jordanian radar. Still they flew west, Egypt nearly 100 miles to the south, past the Nile Delta, past Alexandria. Then, and only then, did they turn toward land in a wide banking curve that brought them into Egypt from the west, flashing over the desert sands toward their targets, flying lower still to elude Egyptian radar. It cost them speed and 30 minutes of fuel. But they won the surprise they sought.

Egyptian planes were on the ground still, and the neat rows made easy, economical targets. Coming in, the Israeli pilots lowered their landing gear to slow their speed and give them more time on target. And they seldom missed and seldom left craters between targets. They wiped out lines of MIGs by the threes and sixes, caught Russian-built medium bombers in revetments. They hit fuel tanks, trucks and buildings, spraying cannon, machine-gun fire and bombs in pass after pass over the Arab bases. They smashed radar installations. And on the way home they pounded at targets of opportunity, columns of tanks and trucks, entrenched and marching troops, fortifications in the sand and in the mountains. They landed only long enough for fuel, ammunition and new targets. Some pilots flew eight missions the first day—hitting Egypt in the morning, Jordan, Iraq and Syria in the afternoon. One of the prime and early targets was the Jordanian radar station that Egypt-bound attackers had to fly low to elude. It was destroyed.

The Israeli fliers showed superb discipline. One flight of four Super Mystères, ordered to hit a specific Egyptian airfield, took evasive action to avoid a dogfight with two Egyptian MIGs to carry out their assignment.

Only rarely did they meet real opposition. At Inshas, Mystère pilots found Egyptian antiaircraft gunners ready, flew through a storm of fire and flying metal to strafe MIGs on the ground. Out of four attacking planes in one flight, the Egyptian ack-ack smashed one and damaged another.

Sometimes there was little or nothing for succeeding Israeli waves to shoot at. Four Mystères, attacking the military field at Fayid near the Suez Canal, destroyed some 18 planes on the ground in their first attack. Ordered back less than two hours later, they could find nothing left but destruction. The same flight was then ordered to attack Amman, the capital of Jordan, and found only one plane left—a Hawker Hunter jet on the ground at the still-smoking airfield. They destroyed it.

It was the final blow for Jordan's puny air force. The waves of Mirages and Mystères now ruled the air over Amman, flying lower than the minarets from which the muezzin call the devout to prayer. From the city's tallest minaret, a loudspeaker boomed: "God is great. Come to pray and greet Mohammed the Prophet." The voice was lost in the roar of Israeli jets banking over the city.

By noon, four hours after his ringing battle order called on the fliers to scatter the enemy in the wilderness, Brigadier Mordechai Hod reported his jets had destroyed more than 400 Arab planes in the air and at 25 fields in four Arab countries. They had also smashed air base and radar installations. The cost—only 19 aircraft lost, all of them over Egypt.

In barely three hours the Israeli surprise attack broke the back of Arab air power, stripped the Arab cities and their troops and tanks and artillery of air cover for the days to come.

Whatever was left of the Arab air forces tried to strike back between noon and 3 P.M. They hit Haifa, the northern port and refinery city. They hit Tiberias in Galilee. Three Syrian MIGs struck at Megiddo in northern Israel. Two were shot down. Other planes hit the coastal resort of Netanya, 43 miles north of Tel Aviv. Six persons were hurt.

By 6 P.M., the Israelis had complete con-

Gingerly the Israeli tanks looked over a dune. And then another. And another.

trol of the air over all fronts. They switched assigned targets from air bases to close support of tanks and infantry. And the targets were easy to find outlined against the severe beige sand of the Sinai. The Israeli jets pounded away night and day at Arab Legion positions in the Jordanian hills around Jerusalem. They answered Syrian artillery with bomb attacks on the mountains. In the open desert nothing could move or hide during the day without detection from the air. The jets ranged as far south as Sharm el Sheikh at the mouth of the Gulf of Aqaba, the narrow exit to the sea that Nasser hoped to make his own. They struck at dug-in Egyptian tanks and artillery at Abu Ageila, Bir Gifgafa, El Kuntilla, El Arish and El Quseima. By nightfall, Egyptian troops in the line, already pounded by airborne fragmentation bombs and burning white phosphorus and napalm, were asking over and over, "Where are our planes?" There were none that belonged to them.

■ Now the fire was lit from the sparks of ancient enmity. Now the Middle East exploded in the hungry flames that were to devour the fortunes of five nations and leave their borders charred and indefinite. Israeli troops blazed across the Sinai against Egypt. In the east, other Israeli forces hesitated and then smashed into Jordan in three drives to silence the Arab Legion guns chipping away at Jerusalem and Tel Aviv. And in the north, ominously, the mountains of Syria rumbled with artillery fire sent crashing into the oldest communal farms of Israel, huddled along the border. It all began in the morning where the reddish desert poinsettias in the Gaza Strip waited for the first light.

On the sands of the Negev, the Sinai and Gaza, June 5 began cold and quiet. But about 4 A.M., mortar shells began dropping again into kibbutzim from the Gaza Strip, the sort of harassment that from week to week shook the uneasy truce from both sides. Again, the *chavarim* (comrades) of the communal farms sent their families to

shelters and took defensive positions on the perimeters. No one was hurt. Only an episode? Perhaps.

Farther behind the border, the Israeli ground forces were waiting. The nation that drives its taxicabs and its farm trucks to war was ready.

Finally the orders came. A radio in a command car stabbed out the electric words. A line of tanks moved forward. "*Kadima* (Let's go)," shouted an officer in Hebrew. It had begun.

The Israeli battle plan quickly became clear: drive three steel fists westward across the Sinai to close the three main gates to Egypt proper—the Mitla Pass in the south, Bir Gifgafa in the middle, El Qantara on the coast road in the north. For insurance, the Israelis unleashed a quick, light jab across the southern desert to guarantee the Mitla Pass would be sealed quickly. Between these portals to Egypt from the Sinai wilderness lay mountains and impassable dunes, tough going even for men on foot, impossible for vehicles.

The object: to bottle up the 100,000 Egyptians and their equipment in the burning desert without water and supplies, and thus destroy a third of Nasser's army. To take the Sinai and thus remove the Egyptian threat to the Gulf of Aqaba. The tactics—speed and encirclement; bypass strong points if necessary, mop them up later. The forces—three spearheads, each with its own armor and artillery, each an independent task force capable of operating on the desert for several days without resupply.

Brigadier Israel Tal, commander of the northern drive, knew he would have to break through at Khan Yunis, cutting off the Gaza Strip. He would send infantry and tanks north to deal with the Palestinian Liberation Army holding Gaza town and Ali Muntar. His main column would dash along the coast road westward toward the main objective, El Qantara and the northern escape route to Egypt. Brigadier Tal knew this first test with the Egyptians was crucial, not only in terms of time, but for the morale of his soldiers. Orders were to press the attack regardless of casualties.

56

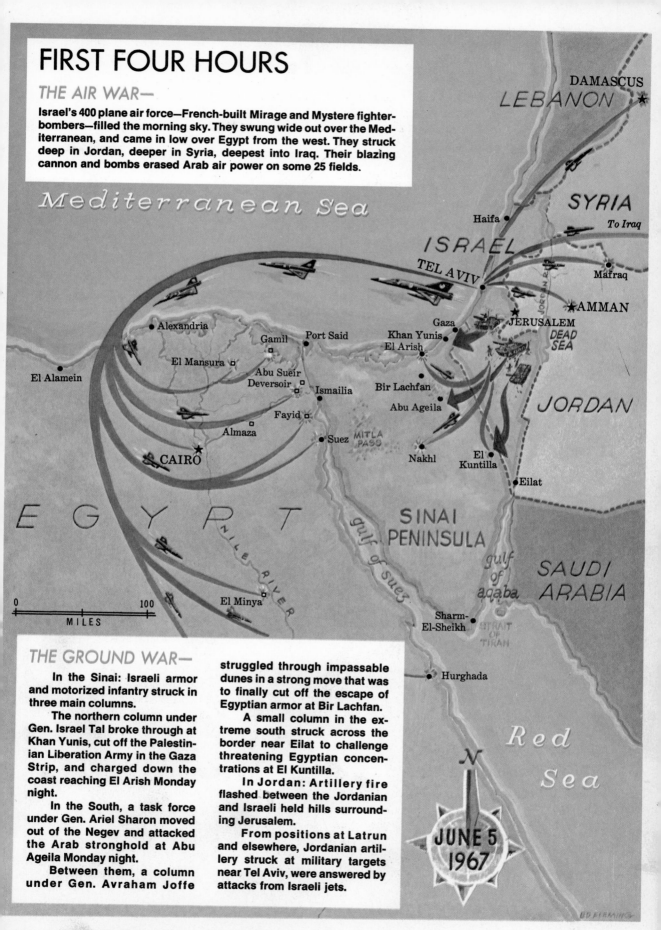

FIRST FOUR HOURS

THE AIR WAR—

Israel's 400 plane air force—French-built Mirage and Mystere fighter-bombers—filled the morning sky. They swung wide out over the Mediterranean, and came in low over Egypt from the west. They struck deep in Jordan, deeper in Syria, deepest into Iraq. Their blazing cannon and bombs erased Arab air power on some 25 fields.

Mediterranean Sea

DAMASCUS
LEBANON
SYRIA
To Iraq
Haifa
ISRAEL
Mafraq
TEL AVIV
Gaza
AMMAN
Khan Yunis
JERUSALEM
El Arish
DEAD SEA
Bir Lachfan
JORDAN
Abu Ageila
Nakhl
El Kuntilla
Eilat

Alexandria
Gamil
Port Said
El Mansura
Abu Sueir
Deversoir
Ismailia
El Alamein
Fayid
Almaza
Suez
MITLA PASS
CAIRO

EGYPT
gulf of suez
SINAI PENINSULA
gulf of aqaba
SAUDI ARABIA

NILE RIVER

El Minya

0   100
MILES

Sharm-El-Sheikh
STRAIT OF TIRAN

Hurghada

N

Red Sea

JUNE 5 1967

THE GROUND WAR—

In the Sinai: Israeli armor and motorized infantry struck in three main columns.

The northern column under Gen. Israel Tal broke through at Khan Yunis, cut off the Palestinian Liberation Army in the Gaza Strip, and charged down the coast reaching El Arish Monday night.

In the South, a task force under Gen. Ariel Sharon moved out of the Negev and attacked the Arab stronghold at Abu Ageila Monday night.

Between them, a column under Gen. Avraham Joffe struggled through impassable dunes in a strong move that was to finally cut off the escape of Egyptian armor at Bir Lachfan.

A small column in the extreme south struck across the border near Eilat to challenge threatening Egyptian concentrations at El Kuntilla.

In Jordan: Artillery fire flashed between the Jordanian and Israeli held hills surrounding Jerusalem.

From positions at Latrun and elsewhere, Jordanian artillery struck at military targets near Tel Aviv, were answered by attacks from Israeli jets.

It didn't seem the Israelis could miss the parked planes . . .

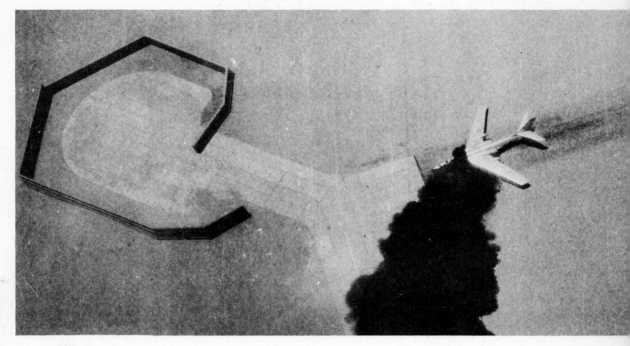

. . . They didn't.

First were the extensive fields of Egyptian mines, made of plastic to foil mine detectors. Beyond, two brigades of Egyptians, dug in, with tanks and artillery.

Brigadier Tal concentrated his artillery on a swath only half a mile wide. The guns barked in rapid fire. The systematic barrage blasted through the scrubby, heavily mined strip. The air trembled with the boom and the sandy earth leaped up in the distance as the concussion detonated the mines. The barrage got most of them, but not all.

Sand-colored tanks and half-tracks pushed out of waiting stations in orange groves and from among the sparse shade trees. Infantrymen in khaki brought up bazookas and machine guns. Tankers in olive green battened down the hatches of the British-built Centurions, the American-made Super Shermans and Pattons, the light French AMX-13s. The lumbering tanks followed the barrage as it inched through the minefields.

Ahead were the sun-baked Arab towns of Khan Yunis and Rafah with their square clay-brick houses and lopsided windows, and wandering camels and dogs suddenly caught up in a war. Israeli soldiers joked about the dogs—"mobile Arab C-rations," they called them.

Then the Israelis broke through, smashed into Khan Yunis within hours of the battle's beginning, drove on to Rafah. Before the towns were even secured, Israeli tanks had begun plunging westward toward the ultimate objective along the coast road. Now Brigadier Tal sent infantry and tanks north up the road to Gaza.

A tall Israeli colonel let his binoculars fall loose from the strap around his neck. "You know," he said, "if it weren't for those 200,000 Palestine Arab refugees over there, we could just throw in everything we have and knock out the Egyptians in no time."

The Israeli tankers were already on their way, pounding down the coast road, their vanguard already miles ahead. They swept through small Egyptian towns along the way pausing only long enough to deal with the light opposition. By nightfall, they had covered 30 miles and reached El Arish.

Israeli prize: an abandoned caravan of Egyptian armor.

The Suez Canal was less than 100 miles ahead. So fast had the northern drive moved that paratroopers slated to be dropped on El Arish in support were reassigned to other objectives in the rapidly widening war.

The main drive to the south was commanded by Brigadier Ariel Sharon. He faced Egyptian fortifications in depth aimed at the Negev. They had been reinforced recently with an Egyptian infantry brigade, about ninety tanks and six battalions of artillery. They were dug in and difficult. Some had been sent from Cairo barely three weeks before. Many had come into the line expecting to attack Israel, and were told they would wait for the Israelis to strike the first blow.

Brigadier Sharon's immediate goal was to confront the Egyptians in the Abu Ageila area, then head southwest to El Quseima linking up with the light brigades there for the dash to the Mitla Pass and points south.

The first Israeli blow came from the skies.

Jets hit the well-protected Egyptians with bombs, napalm, machine-gun fire and white phosphorus, which scatters and burns everything it touches. Then tanks probed the Egyptian positions, and the Egyptians took their toll. But protected as they were, the Egyptians had no mobility. To protect themselves from air attacks, they became stuck in the sand. The Israelis began moving around them.

The battle against the Arab stronghold was finally joined in fierce terms Monday night. Paratroopers attacked enemy artillery from the rear while tanks and infantry assaulted the front and flanks. The fighting continued through the night.

Between Brigadier Sharon and Brigadier Tal, the Sinai was considered impassable—great rolling dunes that had been an effective barrier to the heavy vehicles of modern warfare, and a plague for men on foot. Into this no-man's-land, the Israelis launched their third major drive under the command

60

End of the road at the Mitla Pass.

of Brigadier Avraham Joffe. His immediate objective was to drive across the sands and cut off the retreat route for Egyptian tanks at Bir Lachfan, south of El Arish. He was also to plunge southwestward to attack Abu Ageila from the north. His ultimate objective was to drive across the desert to the Mitla Pass and Bir Gifgafa.

The two brigades in the extreme south held down large Egyptian tank forces at Wadi Kureya that threatened to advance into the Negev, apparently to cut off the Aqaba port of Eilat. They also captured Egyptian positions at El Kuntilla before Monday ended.

Across the breadth of the sands, the battle had been joined and the Israeli forces were heavily engaged through the night. Brigadier Tal's troops were now embattled at El Arish. But, nevertheless, they detached troops and tanks southward to join with Brigadier Joffe's forces plunging toward Bir Lachfan. The tactic of encirclement was al-

ready forming not only around specific strongholds such as Abu Ageila and El Kuntilla, but around the entire first line of Egyptian defense along the Negev-Sinai border. When the Egyptians finally did wake up to the need for withdrawal, they would find their rear crawling with Israeli tanks and troops. And the Israeli jets that pounded them mercilessly Monday would make movement almost impossible Tuesday. At dawn, the Egyptians would find themselves in the grim position of having to leap from the frying pan of their strongholds into the fire of the open desert tended by Israeli jets.

More than 150 miles to the north, the mountains of Syria, snow-streaked even on this day of June 5, stared down with menace at the valleys of Israel. Then, suddenly, the mountains boomed with a lethal voice and shells from Syrian artillery rained down on the communal farms of Israel again. For the *chavarim* it might have been like

61

any of the harassing attacks of the last months. But this one was different. This one, they knew, was war.

At Degania, the oldest kibbutz in Israel, the kibbutz of heroic Moshe Dayan, of revered David Ben-Gurion, once again the women herded the children into the shelters. The young men and the old men, the ones who had not left to go to war, hauled the machine guns from the ammunition shed. War had come to them. They dug new bunkers, set defense assignments. The first Syrian artillery rounds fell in artificial ponds where the farmers were raising carp to process into gefüllte fish.

To the south, where the hills of Jordan and Israel embrace Jerusalem, there was the smallest hope that the city would be spared the ravages of combat. It had been the least violent of borders—until the previous November, when Israeli marauders leveled the village of Es Samu in retaliation for a Syrian commando raid. That act tied Jordan's fortunes to those of the bellicose Arab world. Still, this morning of June 5, there was hope Jordan's King Hussein and his tough Arab Legion would not go to war.

That hope perished with the crash of artillery about 10:30 A.M. Jordanian guns in the hills around Jerusalem pummeled the Israeli New City of Jerusalem. Israeli artillery slugged back. Jordanian guns at Latrun, which could reach the sea across the 14-mile waist of Israel, began picking out targets near Tel Aviv on the coast, the airport at Lod, and various supply points. One shell fell on Tel Aviv itself, wrecking two apartments in a four-story building.

So it began—and with it Israeli plans for sweeping the Jordanians back across the River Jordan. This slice of the war, the slowest to start, would become the first to end. But it was to be bloody, bloodier hour for hour than any of the others, as Israeli forces formed a giant pincers over the Jordanian bulge and a smaller one in the hills around Jerusalem.

The Arab Legion moved quickly. It seized the palace of the high commissioner, a relic of the British mandate that had been taken over by the UN Truce Supervisory Organization. The Israelis struck back. A reconnaissance unit of the Jerusalem Brigade spearheaded the attack and the fighting was fierce. At length the Jordanian troops fell back in the courtyard of the palace, a jungle of smashed UN vehicles, and by 2 P.M. it was over. A battalion of Israeli infantry now commanded the strategic hill and pressed on to Sur Bahir and Ramat Rahel, other UN outposts south of the Old City.

Now the entire ring of hills around Jerusalem erupted in fire. Israeli tanks plowed through the rubble of the no-man's-land, the corridor, that separated the Jordanian and Israeli sectors of Jerusalem. Both sides exchanged violent mortar barrages from only a few hundred yards range. Some frontline positions were barely 10 yards apart. The Israelis moved in reinforcements, brought up more artillery. The Arab Legionnaires, many of whom had fought on the same ground and through the same houses in 1948, dug in, ready to resist assaults on the Mandelbaum and Damascus gates to the city. The fighting began as it had begun 19 years before: house by house, street by street, hand to hand. But this time there was an added and decisive ingredient. At noon, Israeli jets flashed over the city, pounding the right flank of the Jordanians on high ground to the north. Then they dropped napalm. One napalm bomb landed in the courtyard of the Al Aqsa mosque in the Haram el Sharif section that held within its walls both the Dome of the Rock, sacred to Moslems, and the remnant of the Second Temple of Solomon, the Wailing Wall, sacred to Jews. The Israeli air power took a steadily increasing toll of the Jordanian forces. The tiny Jordanian air force was destroyed in the first hours.

Darkness came, and with it attacks by Israeli tanks and motorized infantry. The front lines changed hands several times in the clash of attack and counterattack. But the Israelis were not concerning themselves with Jerusalem alone. Tanks also attacked the outlying hills, seeking the commanding heights. They struck north and south, silencing the guns at Latrun, beginning a drive for Ramallah, and a swing toward Bethlehem. Smoke wreathed the border area and Mount Zion, the site of King David's Tomb. Artillery bursts broke on Mount Scopus, an Israeli enclave within the Jordanian sector where only Israeli police had been allowed since the Jordanians cut off Israeli travel to the university and hospital on the heights.

By midnight, Sheik Aziz had fallen to the Israelis and the pincers was beginning to tighten around the city. New assault troops readied themselves for the attack on the old city.

To the north of the Jordanian bulge, near Jenin, Israeli tanks battled their way to commanding heights over the town. Israeli infantry made a feint toward the south to hide the main attack that was to break in the early hours of Tuesday.

In what was to be the final front in the war, the pattern was already established. Jordanian soldiers, from the hills of Jerusalem to the shores of Galilee, were already hard-pressed by Israeli tanks and jet firepower. Iraqi troops, long promised, were not in sight. Saudi Arabian reinforcements, reportedly two weeks en route, were not heard from. King Hussein's tough Legionnaires would have to go it alone. Without air cover, without real hope.

But Israeli hearts were concentrating on one front—Jerusalem, where stood the Wailing Wall, barred to them for 2,000 years. And Jews there, and Jews everywhere, were voicing the ancient hope with new excitement: "Next year in Jerusalem."

Next month? Next week? Tomorrow?

■In the cities of the nations now at war, there was, at first, surprise, disbelief, a feeling of remoteness.

The air raid sirens shrieked first in Cairo at 9 A.M. and 15 minutes later brown puffs of Egyptian antiaircraft fire stained the sky. Israeli planes were attacking airports around Nasser's capital.

Traffic stopped as people gawked at the heavens and clustered around public loud-speakers mounted in the streets and in the squares. "Our armies have only one cry," shouted Cairo Radio. "To Tel Aviv! One Arab army! One Arab nation! . . . 24 jets have been downed . . ." Then 46 and 60 and more, and Egyptians thought they were winning the war. The crowds went wild with cheering, danced in the streets, yelling "On to Tel Aviv! One man turned from his radio and said, "Helas Tel Aviv" (Tel Aviv is finished). A pretty girl flexed her arm at a foreigner and smiled, "We are very strong," she said.

Mobs roamed the streets. American cameramen trying to film the scene were attacked. Anti-American and anti-Israeli posters were showing up everywhere, it seemed. Riot police moved in to guard the U. S. Embassy and the gates were locked with heavy chains. All through the day Cairo Radio stoked the emotional fires and all through the day antiaircraft guns thundered at the sky. No bombs were dropped on populated civilian areas. Cairo airport closed and incoming flights of TWA and Olympic Airways were radioed back to Athens.

An Israeli plane, hit by antiaircraft fire, fell in flames in the center of the city. A crowd gathered around quickly, shouting, "Nasser! Nasser!"

In "finished" Tel Aviv, children were filling sandbags and adults were painting their car headlights blue in anticipation of the blackout. Between air alerts, people gathered in the streets in front of supermarkets, parked taxis, buses and doorsteps to listen to news, folk songs and martial music. Kol Yisrael, the official radio, summoned remaining reserve units by code name: "Wedding March . . . Alternating Current . . . Men At Work . . . Close Shave . . . Open Window . . . Good Friends . . ." Throughout the tiny nation men were scrambling off to war. Some reserve units called into action got more than a 100 percent return on the summons as men over 49, legally too old, showed up with their old outfits anyway.

A prisoner in the city jail, convicted of robbery, had been given the weekend off to visit his family. When the call to arms came, he went directly to his reserve outfit, not the jail.

In Haifa, a cab driver heard his unit called, stopped in front of a hotel on Mount Carmel, reached into the trunk of the car for his helmet, sleeping bag and submachine gun, turned down his sun visor to display an "off duty" sign and drove off to war.

In Amman, King Hussein declared martial law. Schools closed. Ambulances dashed through the city streets. Only Israeli jets were seen overhead, and the day rang with air raid sirens. In a message to his people, Jordan's 31-year-old monarch said: "We are on the threshold of the final battle, and we hope that God will grant us victory. We are determined to live nobly, or die."

In Damascus, Israeli jets swept over the city for more than three hours, spitting rockets and machine-gun fire. Called the oldest inhabited city in the world, Damascus is a cluster of gardens and orchards, mosques and minarets astride the Barada River. Now Syrians stood in open doorways, and the shelter of the ancient walls of the old city to watch the antiaircraft dot the sky. Some storekeepers kept their shops open despite the raids. And along the timeworn streets that lead to Mecca, Syrian fathers lugged suitcases and mothers herded their children along, moving from their homes to the protection of shelters in big modern buildings of the new city. Smoke rose from three corners of the city.

But no city was as close to the war as the "City of Peace," Jerusalem.

Mrs. Anna Eiges, the wife of a doctor, left a Jerusalem supermarket where she had been shopping when the first air raid alert sounded. She headed toward a shelter and met an elderly neighbor coming in the opposite direction toward the government buildings at the bottom of the hill.

"Where are you going, Esther?" she asked.

"To pay my municipal taxes."

"At a time like this?"

"Well, they might need the money." The old lady marched off down the street, stopped finally by a policeman who herded her into

a shelter under the bus station where she spent the next seven hours, her tax money still clutched in her hand.

Jossi Stern, one of Israel's leading artists, was in his studio overlooking the domes and minarets and steeples of the Old City of Jerusalem when a telephone call summoned him to duty as a combat artist. He was working on an oil of Joseph, The Dreamer, the Hebrew boy who in the Old Testament was sold into captivity by his jealous brothers and ended up interpreting the dreams of the Pharaoh of Egypt.

Jossi Stern couldn't believe that war had come again to Israel. "Not in the age of the United Nations, with great powers like Russia and the United States looking on," he told his mother. But, off to war he went for

Israeli guns pound the road to Suez.

the third time in his life, wearing a khaki shirt from the days of the British Mandate, trousers from the War of Independence in 1948, a cap from the 1956 war, and his own shoes, a pair of open sandals. Before noon he was at work in the same printshop where he had worked in the 1948 war on "Combat Page," a four-page collection of humorous articles, cartoons and puzzles for troops in the field. The work was interrupted by alerts that sent him and his staff to the shelter, and they missed an issue the next day when the printer was wounded by shells raining down from the Jordanian hills around the city.

Kol Yisrael quickly changed its programming from American and British mod music, the Beatles and the Supremes, to national music. Many learned, for the first time, all the words to *Hatikvah,* the Israeli national anthem. But the most popular song was *Jerusalem the Golden,* sung by Hadassah Sigalov and soldiers stationed in the hills waiting to take the Old City. Composer Naomi Shemer wrote new lyrics that sang of this war and 2,000 years of Jewish hopes and dreams and yearning.

Kol Yisrael's radio reports on the war were calm and detailed, in sharp contrast to the boastings of Arab television and radio stations received in Israel, which has no television station of its own. Israelis could sit in coffee shops and hotel lobbies to see TV Cairo and TV Damascus commentators tell how Haifa was overrun, Tel Aviv was wiped out, Jerusalem was burned. The

65

Arabs, telecasting in atrocious Hebrew, preached the propaganda to the Israelis and provided the only laughs in the tensions of war. But one night, TV Cairo showed a picture of a downed Israeli pilot in the Sinai hacked to death when he pulled his gun on a group of Egyptian farmers armed with the pickaxes they use to till the earth. The fun was gone.

Prominent on a high terraced hill in the New City is the Hadassah-Hebrew University Medical Center, the biggest hospital in the Middle East. What was left of its staff, after mobilization, put into effect a pre-arranged emergency plan to prepare for the expected flood of casualties. Hallways were converted to receiving wards, and helicopter landing areas were cleared on the lawn.

Architect Dan Ben-Dor rushed to the hospital to help salvage the center's most coveted art treasure, the world-famous Chagall stained glass windows in the Hospital Synagogue, each depicting one of the Twelve Tribes of Israel. The French firm that executed Marc Chagall's brilliant splashes of color designed the windows so they could be removed in an hour. Ben-Dor had the original wooden cases brought up from the basement for quick re-storage. To his dismay, he discovered that the putty around the windows had hardened in the hot sun and dry air, and each window would have to be cut away from its leaden frame. There was no time to await the arrival of an expert, so he did it himself with a jeweler's carborundum saw.

He was still working on the first window when the artillery fire began from the Jordanian hills that look down on the hospital complex. He hurried to the shelter. A few minutes later a shell landed in the concrete courtyard between the maternity clinic and the synagogue and shrapnel damaged two of the windows. Ben-Dor went back to work at noon, patching the damaged windows with Scotch tape and trying to remove the others while the artillery continued to sound from the hills. In the next two and a half days he was able to remove only nine of the windows.

"Wars you have every day," architect

Ben-Dor said, "but only once in the history of the world do you get windows like these." From his home in France artist Chagall wired: "I am not worried about the windows, only about the safety of Israel. Let Israel be safe and I will make you better windows."

As the ferocity of the fighting in the hills grew, the hospital was swamped with casualties. During one lull, Dr. Jack Karpas looked out at the heights of a round hilltop called Castel where Roman legions once had a fort, and saw Israeli tanks stymied by Jordanian artillery. Later he learned that his son, Sergeant Charles Karpas, a tank commander, was in the column and spent the night on the mountain.

Another doctor looked out of the window during a lull in the shelling and saw a crater where his car had been parked. In

his mind he wrote off the $5,000 the war had suddenly cost him.

All the embattled cities of the Middle East blacked out Monday night. In Cairo, young Futuwa units in blue-gray uniforms patrolled the streets and shouted blackout orders at the slightest glint of light. In Tel Aviv, the skyline was faint against the moonless night, and wardens broke into one shop where a careless storekeeper left a light burning. Only in Jerusalem were there lights where the yellow and orange artillery bursts sparked across the Judean hills, and flares and searchlights helped the Israeli air force find targets around but not in the precious Old City.

Already there were subtle changes in mood and feeling about the war. In Israel the people heard that the Arab air forces had been destroyed, that their own troops were advancing in the Sinai and the Jordanian bulge—and they dreamed, dared to dream, of walking through old Jerusalem again.

In Cairo, there was a discomforting silence about the action in the Sinai. Radio reports claimed more and more Israeli planes shot down, but still they filled the air over Egypt. Why? What could have happened? The morning's confidence vanished. And already people were thinking of reasons. A rumor of U.S. intervention—only a will-o'-the-wisp rumor—grew stronger in Amman and Cairo, so strong that British intelligence picked it up. And so strong that the U.S. Defense Department denied what it called "reports" of intervention.

And at Hadassah Hospital the casualties

Israeli jets flew lower than the minarets, and smoke rose over Amman.

of the Jerusalem fighting swelled. Ambulances seemed to arrive every few seconds. Dentists and students were mobilized as anesthetists. Even the basement was converted into a receiving ward. The wounded, mostly paratroopers, buried their faces in their pillows and bit their lips lest they betray their pain. Among the wounded were soldiers of Jordan's Arab Legion, treated side by side in the corridor emergency wards with Israeli wounded. One Legionnaire had lost an eye and could barely see out of the other. He kept muttering in Hebrew to the young Israeli paratrooper on the litter next to him: "Brothers, we are brothers."

■ The moon lit the White House, the sun, the Kremlin when the word flashed around the globe. Five bells rang on teletype machines in Washington:

BULLETIN

JERUSALEM (AP) — An Israeli Army spokesman announced that heavy fighting has broken out between Egyptian and Israeli forces. . . .

One minute after the dispatch cleared the wire, at 2:50 A.M. Eastern Daylight Time, the telephone rang at the bedside of Walt W. Rostow, President Lyndon Johnson's Special Assistant for National Security Affairs. Other phone calls snaked out across the darkened city. Officials sat up in bed, rubbed their eyes, flipped on radios.

As the crisis in the Middle East had grown daily more taut, like a violin string drawn inexorably tighter, both Washington and Moscow were acutely aware that one accidental turn of the screw, one small diplomatic miscalculation, could bring the world's two great nuclear powers to a confrontation both wished desperately to avoid. Now the string had snapped. Now, in yet another grim repetition of history unlearned, passion had betrayed reason and men were killing men.

Walt Rostow dressed. In 35 minutes he was poring over dispatches in the top secret, map-lined Situation Room in the White House basement, the President's personal command post.

At the State Department, where only the windows of the Operations Center on the seventh floor showed light, the duty officer placed a call to the home of Secretary of State Dean Rusk in suburban Spring Valley. While the Secretary dressed, Mrs. Rusk, an understanding veteran of crisis, put on a pot of coffee and fixed a plate of poached eggs and sausage. Ignoring his chauffeur and bodyguards, the secretary climbed into the family Ford and drove alone to his office through the dark and empty streets.

At 4:30 A.M. Rostow decided to awaken the President. Instantly alert, Mr. Johnson began issuing orders. Flicking remote control switches from his carved wooden bedstead, he tuned in radio and television reports which at that hour provided more information than official embassy dispatches. By phone, he instructed Secretary Rusk to arrange for an early briefing of congressional leaders. Over a bedside breakfast of grapefruit and chipped beef, he drafted a public statement deploring the war and calling on support of the United Nations in bringing about a cease-fire. One by one lights flickered on in offices all over town. By the time the first pearl-gray light appeared official Washington was stirring as though it were midday.

So, presumably, was official Moscow, where indeed it was midday. For, to the utter astonishment of Rostow and his staff in the Situation Room, a certain closely-guarded, continuously-monitored teletype machine suddenly came to life. The Kremlin was calling.

Never before, since it was installed during the administration of President John Kennedy, had the legendary "hot line" been put to use for its intended purpose: to offer instant and direct dialogue at a time of world crisis. Now its worth became instantly established. In carefully drawn sentences, Soviet Premier Alexei Kosygin let President Johnson know that his country did not want war in the Middle East and that perhaps the world's two superpowers might work together to help restore peace.

President Johnson, still in his bedroom, lost no time in drafting a reply.

Throughout the day, conference rooms all over town buzzed with taut, high-level discussion.

The President called an early morning meeting with Rostow, Secretary Rusk, Secretary of Defense Robert McNamara and others to discuss ways to win agreement with the Soviets and gain a cease-fire resolution in the UN. To a later meeting, he summoned additional brainpower—former Secretary of State Dean Acheson; Clark Clifford, the Chairman of the Foreign Intelligence Advisory Board; McGeorge Bundy, who once held Rostow's job; Llewellyn Thompson, the Ambassador to Moscow, who happened to be in town. Another meeting was with the Secretary of the Treasury and other financial and economic specialists. So it went through the day. During one two-hour period Mr. Johnson received four phone calls and placed 22.

Just after noon, a crisis-within-a-crisis developed. Explaining the U.S. position in the war, Robert J. McCloskey, the State Department press officer, said the United States was "neutral in thought, word and deed." Did this mean, then, that the U.S. was backing down from its position that the Gulf of Aqaba should be an open waterway? Reporters were asking. The President, annoyed, summoned Secretary Rusk. He met with the Secretary for 27 minutes, then sent him to explain to newsmen that the United States was "nonbelligerent," but hardly indifferent.

Great Britain took similar pains to proclaim its impartiality. In the House of Commons, Foreign Secretary George Brown declared: "British concern is not to take sides. Instructions are being given to all our forces in the area to avoid any involvement in the conflict." Earlier in the day, Brown had met separately with the American, French and Soviet ambassadors and proposed a three-point approach toward a settlement. He wanted all the big powers to agree to keep out of the fighting, quit delivering arms to the combatants, and back a Security Council resolution for a cease-fire.

The Russian ambassador gave Mr. Brown no indication of how Moscow would react. In the Soviet capital, official broadcasts throughout the day stressed "resolute support" for the Arabs and demanded that Israel pull back her troops.

It was not in Washington, Moscow or London, however, but at United Nations headquarters in New York, that the great diplomatic drama would unfold. Since its founding at the end of World War II, the UN Security Council had met more times over Middle Eastern crises than any other. Now, once again, the Council faced a Middle Eastern problem, this one graver than ever before.

The president of the 15-member Security Council for the month of June, Hans Tabor of Denmark, learned of the fighting at 3:10 A.M. with a phone call from Israeli Ambassador Gideon Raphael, who said the Arabs had attacked his country. Twenty minutes later Egyptian Ambassador Mohamed Awad el Kony phoned and claimed the Israelis had attacked *his* country. Tabor notified Secretary-General U Thant. The Security Council convened at 10:21 A.M.

Secretary-General Thant reported to the delegates what information he had learned from UN sources at the battlefront, but at that hour news was fragmentary. Ambassadors Raphael and El Kony both spoke, each accusing the other's country of starting the war. At 11:15 A.M. President Tabor suspended the meeting. He decided that private consultations over a cease-fire proposal would accomplish more than Council debate.

For 11 hours, ambassadors from the various nations huddled and parleyed, telephoned and cabled. The aim, of course, was to draft a resolution that the Council would accept and the warring countries would obey. It soon became clear that wouldn't be easy. The Soviet bloc and the Arab states insisted that both sides withdraw to the positions they held June 4, the day before the fighting began. But the United States and Britain felt this would appear to condone Egypt's blockade of the Gulf of Aqaba. Impasse. At length Tabor reconvened the Council at 10:20 P.M. and asked the members if they would agree to adjourn and try again tomorrow. They agreed.

■ In the wilderness of Paran, where Ishmael, ancestor of all Arabs, once dwelt for 40 years, where, at another time in the ancient past, the Children of Israel trudged in their journey to the Promised Land, dawn roused the parched village of El Kuntilla and the mighty Egyptian encampment there. It was Monday, June 5. Corporal Kamal Mahrouss, the farmer's son, anticipated yet another routine day for his infantry unit.

The message came over field radios at 9 A.M. The war was on! Corporal Mahrouss and his comrades raised a cheer. "Let's march on Israel now!" some cried. But their orders were not to attack.

El Kuntilla lay on the border between the Sinai and the Negev deserts, the dividing line between Egypt and Israel. It controlled the passage from Israel to Sharm el Sheikh at the mouth of the Gulf of Aqaba. Any Israeli troops headed by land to that strategic port city would have to get past El Kuntilla, past the entrenched Egyptian guns trained point-blank at the Israeli border.

At 9:15 A.M. Corporal Mahrouss saw the Israeli planes coming. They flashed high out of the desert sun, beyond the reach of anti-aircraft fire, and passed directly overhead. Then they turned around, dived, and streaked in low over the dunes from the west, hitting the eastward-aimed Egyptian guns from behind.

Again and again they struck. Corporal Mahrouss, firing furiously with his rifles, saw four Israeli planes fall. Bombs exploded all around but the Egyptian troops were dug in well and casualties were light. It was clear to Corporal Mahrouss that the Israeli airmen were concentrating on equipment and munitions dumps. Their aim was good.

"Where are our planes? Where are our planes?" Everyone asked the same frantic question but no answer came.

And when night fell, around the sands of El Kuntilla lay the wreckage of half the

70

The Israeli breakthrough in the Gaza Strip, a swathe of death and destruction.

Egyptian unit's equipment and supplies. That night Corporal Kamal Mahrouss did not sleep after the first day of the war for which he had been so impatient.

■ The jets flashed over Wadi el Arish while Colonel Mohamed Galal and the officers on his Egyptian artillery brigade staff were finishing breakfast on this Monday morning. They came out of the sun, four camouflaged Mystères, and by Colonel Galal's estimate weren't more than 650 feet above the valley. They flew right past, ignoring Gala's brigade and its 36 well-entrenched howitzers pointing toward the Israeli border 37 miles eastward across the Sinai sands.

"Whose were they?" an officer asked.

"Israelis," said Colonel Galal. "Probably on a reconnaisance mission."

Moments later antiaircraft fire rattled to the rear, near the Egyptian supply dump at Bir Hasana, and smoke spiraled skyward. It was no reconnaisance mission. Colonel Galal rang his officers. All were at their posts. He drove to his observation post, five and a half miles south, where he could get a good view east. Thirty miles in that direction was El Quseima, where the first line of Egyptian troops were arrayed at the frontier.

A second wave of Israeli jets flashed overhead, this time 12 of them. They peeled off, fired four rockets each and headed back home. The attacks continued at 90-minute intervals and dark smoke clouded the blue desert sky above the supply dump.

"Where are *our* planes?" a junior officer asked the colonel.

"Probably fighting in front of us," Galal replied.

At midday the attacking fighters hit rear elements of Galal's unit. From the observation post he could see one truck in flames and learned that two or three more had been hit but there were no casualties.

Near sundown the attacks slackened as Colonel Galal was summoned to a staff meeting. Standing in the open, on a desert rise called Ras Ebeid five miles to the rear,

the commanding general of the Wadi el Arish forces briefed his officers. He told them the Israelis had started the war and were concentrating their attack on airfields, supply dumps and troop assembly areas. Colonal Galal thought that was normal. He assumed Egyptian war planes were doing the same to the Israelis.

The briefing over, Galal grabbed a handful of biscuits, his first food since breakfast, and hurried back to his brigade. He learned that in his absence two men were wounded and nine trucks destroyed.

At nightfall, the attacks ended in the valley but Galal could still hear distant explosions ahead and behind and on his left flank. He gave orders for the night watch, climbed into his lorry and stretched out on the mattress. Lying awake, he tried to anticipate what form an Israeli ground attack might take if one should come, and to figure out a response for each possiblity.

"Whatever happens," thought Colonel Mohamed Galal, "I will hold my position and fight to the last man."

■ Paratroop Captain Matan Goor knew something was going to happen Monday morning when he saw three Israeli jet bombers roar off from the Tel Nov airfield, near where he and the other members of the 55th Parachute Battalion were encamped in the orange grove. It was shortly after 8:30 A.M. and the planes streaked off in a due westerly direction. Gorr and some of the other field grade officers hurried to the command post to listen to the radio reports coming in from the Headquarters Central Command on a special frequency. It was then he learned for the first time that his country was at war.

At 10 A.M. Goor was ordered to get his red berets, as the Israeli paratroopers proudly called themselves, ready for an assault jump into El Arish on the Mediterranean coast of the Sinai Peninsula. The jump was scheduled for 4:30 P.M., and Goor set about handing out maps and aerial photographs of the area. The details of breaking camp, studying the terrain and planning the jump occupied him most of the rest of the morning, but some of the enlisted men kept him posted on the progress of the war by listening to Kol Yisrael on their pocket transistor radios. The captain was shocked and saddened to learn that Jordan, too, had joined the war. He felt some affection for the Jordanians, but little for the Egyptians, whom he had fought before in the Sinai in the 1956 war. That time they had gone in by truck.

Back in his hometown of Pardess Hana, his handsome, brunette wife, Simcha learned of the war when a phone call from the local civil defense told her to stand by for duty as an emergency ambulance driver, if needed. She looked out the window of their lovely home and saw that Ahmad Ben Essa, the Arab laborer who helped out in the little orange grove they had planted, was laying out some irrigation pipe. She wondered if he knew there was a war on.

At the Agricultural Secondary School, where Matan taught biology, the older boys had taken over complete operation of the farm, driving the tractors, milking the dairy herd, bringing in the second of the three harvests that the lush coastal plain is blessed with each year. By now, all the teachers had been called to active duty. At the school for special problem children where she taught, even the seven- and eight-year-olds were digging ditches and filling sandbags.

Captain Goor and his men were packed up and ready to go, waiting for the trucks to take them across the airstrip to the cargo planes from which they would jump, when at 12:30 P.M. their orders were suddenly changed. The air and the tank war was going so well and so swiftly in the Sinai desert that the paratroopers were not needed. Instead, they were alerted for a ground assault on the Old City of Jerusalem. The men cheered the new orders. Like Goor, most of them were not religious Jews, but the Old City of David and Solomon, of Isaiah and Jeremiah had a deep emotional appeal. As Canaanites and Egyptians, Babylonians and Persians, Greeks and Romans, Arabs, Crusaders, Mamelukes, Ottoman

Turks and British Tommies had done in the centuries before them, they were willing to fight and die for it.

For them, the war had now become an *Aliyah,* literally a going up to Jerusalem.

Now new maps and aerial photographs would be needed. As a forward intelligence officer, Goor climbed into a squad car and drove 10 miles northeast to Ramle, headquarters of Aluf Mishne Eliezer Amital, commander of the Jerusalem Brigade. He returned with the maps about 6 P.M., in time to load his men into buses—non-air-conditioned metropolitan buses this time—for the 35-mile trip to Jerusalem. The captain had not eaten all day, but he was not hungry. The adrenalin of action and expectation was thumping through his system, driving away appetite and even fatigue. It was twilight when they arrived on the outskirts of Jerusalem. The mosques and domes and crenelated walls of the Old City rose dimly in the distance. All paratroop commanders were summoned to an immediate staff conference to plan the assault on the Old City.

A three-pronged attack was planned for one hour after midnight. Captain Goor's outfit drew the northern prong—across Mount Scopus and the Mount of Olives and down through the St. Stephen's Gate. Captain Goor still had time to catch a nap before zero hour, but it was too noisy to sleep. Artillery hissed overhead and exploded in cascades of fire in the distance. Mortars thumped constantly. An experienced soldier, Captain Goor could plainly distinguish the rattle of the 50-calibers from the whine of the recoilless rifles and the whoosh of the big guns on the tank turrets. Giant searchlights probed back and forth across the rose-dun walls built by the Turks in the 16th century. Every now and then a fiery explosion brought into harsh silhouette a familiar landmark like David's Tower and the Mosque of Omar.

The night turned cold, as it does this time of year in the Judean hills. A thin, one-third moon rose up over Mount Scopus and seemed to hang over the deserted buildings of its Hebrew University and

Past burning Egyptian trucks, Israeli columns roll on.

Hadassah Hospital, abandoned 19 years ago.

"A Turk's moon," Captain Goor said to one of his sergeants. "What sort of omen do you think that is?"

The sergeant made no answer. Both looked at their watches. Midnight. One hour to go.

Ir Hakodish, the Holy Place, awaited in the distance.

■ To Major Jamil of the Arab Legion, it was only a matter of time. He knew the time had come that morning when he heard on the radio that Israeli jets had raided Egypt.

He knew his turn would be next. So it was.

Both sides began shooting with everything, machine guns, mortars, rifles.

"The Israelis threw a hand grenade at one of the Legion's positions near the Mandelbaum Gate. One of Jamil's men caught it and tried to throw it back. It blew up in his hand and killed him. The Israelis threw a second grenade. Another of Jamil's men managed to return it this time.

At places the two foes were only 10 yards apart. It was like 1948 all over again. Almost. Then there had been no planes. Now Jamil first heard the deadly rush of Israeli jets.

But he and his men held. "We aren't, he said, "going to retreat even the span of a hand." They hoped to enter Jewish Jerusalem and were waiting for the order to advance from minute to minute.

But the minutes passed and no order came. Jamil saw sudden black clouds of oily smoke rise from the battle area. Napalm, he thought. Ammunition began to run low. Jamil sent to the rear for more. Bad news came back. The jets were hitting at Jordanian supply depots. Yes, 1967 was different.

Now, it was one continuous air raid. In 1948 they fought on the ground, street by street.

Night came as the Israelis concentrated artillery fire at the heights around the Ambassador Hotel, in other times one of the best places to view the ancient domes and

75

modern office buildings of the Holy City. Even at night the bombs still fell as Israeli spotlights and flares lit the way for the jets that roared unseen in the dark like a venging angels.

Jamil kept waiting for the word to advance. But the bombing went on and still it did not come.

■ For the more than one million Arab refugees living in UN shanty towns on the perimeter of old Palestine, the war came with a swiftness and a fury that was both terrible and surprising. All week long they had been waiting for war, watching for war, some even hoping for war, in the expectation that an Arab victory might soon return them to the homes they had fled or been forced out of when the State of Israel came into being in 1948.

The displaced persons in Camp Aqabat Jaber, like their Arab brothers in the other UN camps on the west bank of the Jordan River, had seen the Iraqi and Jordanian tanks and half-tracks lumber by on the way to take up positions around Jerusalem. They had waved at the trucks full of soldiers and listened to Nasser promising them deliverance over Cairo Radio.

Then at 9:30 A.M., the war was on their doorstep. Israeli planes, silver slivers in the bright sunlight, came streaking in over the Mountains of Moab. They roared down over the blue-green waters of the Dead Sea and, in wave after wave, strafed and bombed the long line of tanks and trucks stretched out as far as a pilot's eye could see along the main road from Amman to Jerusalem.

Rashid Areikat, the thin, sad-faced Palestine Arab who ran four refugee camps for the United Nations Relief Agency, crouched on the floor of his little office in Camp Aqabat Jaber listening to the planes scream in. In the first hour he counted 20 air strikes. In the next two days, he would count more than 200. Night and day, the planes swept down, so that the whole desert to the south and the mountains to the east were aglow, long after sunset, with burning tanks and trucks. None of the camp buildings was hit, but the roads leading to all of them were blocked with smashed-up equipment and still smoldering tanks.

Areikat wondered how long the war would last and what he would do to feed the more than 50,000 refugees in his care. He estimated he had about a two-months supply of food on hand in his storehouses. Already, some of his refugees were packing up, confident they would soon be moving into the homes and apartments they had abandoned 19 years ago to usurpers belonging to a hated nation that called itself Israel instead of Palestine. A few even had moved up the road, trying to push their cartloads of furniture and clothing in and out among the tank columns. Many of these were killed, caught in the air strikes or hit by pieces of blasted tanks. One family had just ventured a few steps past the gate, when its donkey and cart fell to the same burst of rockets from a diving jet that caught an Iraqi tank.

In pleading tones that brought tears to his melancholy eyes, then in a screaming harangue that left his cheeks livid, Rashid Areikat pleaded with the refugees to remain where they were and take cover. But they were nomads of hope, willing to move in the direction of their displaced dreams, no matter how bitter the path. They kept moving west.

■ Monday morning Gershon Fine was sitting in the tourist restaurant having his second cup of coffee and looking out at the sparkling blue waters of the Sea of Galilee. Lake Tiberias, the Romans called it, but the ancients had called it the Sea of Kinneret, because it was shaped like a *kinnor*, the Hebrew word for harp. A lone speedboat was bouncing along the serene waters. Soon, in a few weeks when the bulk of the tourists arrived, speedboats would be zipping in and out among the fishing fleet, pulling water skiers. All around him other kibbutzniks in their high-crowned "idiot" hats were

At Mitla Pass: One of the gates to home the Israelis closed.

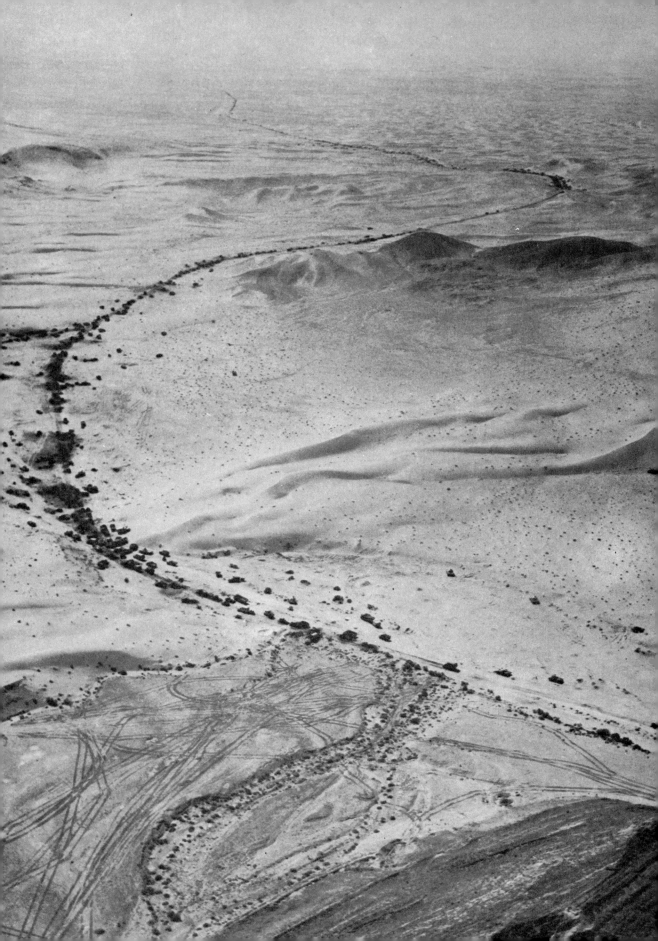

An Egyptian half-track burns on the road to Suez.

having fish for breakfast, St. Peter's fish, a speciality of the house.

It was while walking along these shores, as Fine was fond of telling the tourists, that Jesus saw the brothers Simon, called Peter and Andrew, casting their nets into the sea, and said to them: "Follow me, and I will make you fishers of men."

A Hebrew scholar, Fine liked to let it be known that he was pretty well up on the New Testament, too, although he never allowed a tourist get away without also telling him what the ancient Jewish sages had to say about this lovely lake:

"Jehovah hath created seven seas but the Sea of Galilee is His delight."

It was 8:45 A.M. Most of the younger people already had gone to the fields. An elderly man at the next table was reading a newspaper, discussing now and then the latest Cairo crisis with his tablemates. The waiter was slouched across the counter with a transistor radio held to his ear, suffering through some dreadful mod music, all wailing and high-strung strings, in patient anticipation of the nine o'clock news.

Suddenly the music stopped and a newscaster in a calm, authoritative voice announced that Israel was at war with her Arab neighbors.

Kibbutz Ein Gev responded immediately. After nearly 20 years of almost ceaseless undeclared war, it was more geared for crisis than the rest of the country. Gershon Fine went straightaway to the shelter beneath the rhododendron bushes, where the children of Ein Gev had been sent the previous evening. His emergency assignment was to look after the seven to ten-year-olds, keep them amused, contented, panic-free. Everyone in the Fine family had his own job to do. His wife, Ester, a trained nurse, took care of the underground first aid station, laying out the dressings and bandages, checking on the plasma bottles and penicillin supplies, making sure that the emergency generator was in good working order. Her women friends reported to the dining room to prepare emergency rations for the shelter dwellers.

Twenty-one-year-old Arie, the Fines' oldest boy, grabbed his American-made car-

to 16 explosions. Fox and Arie Fine could count them and hear the earth trembling. They tried to dig the trench deeper as fast as they could. Then they crouched down as far as they could. Fox admitted he was "scared, plenty scared." He had been on hand for the April 7 shelling. On that day, he had just returned from the fields and was putting his tractor into the garage down by the lake. He heard a dull explosion somewhere in the vicinity of the buffer zone of banana trees planted between the buildings and the bombed-out pillbox and thought it might be the sonic boom of a plane streaking out across the lake. Then he saw smoke curling up through the broad-leafed trees, followed by a sudden tongue of flame, and he ran off to the shelter.

This time it was much worse, louder and closer. After the third or fourth set, which crackled like a string of outsize Chinese firecrackers, Fox and his comrades abandoned the trench and made their ways, crouching and running, to the shelter, along little culverts lined with corrugated tin that the kibbutz defense staff had been deepening and improving since the 1948 war.

By now the electricity had been cut off, and the women had left the kitchen to go to the shelters. For the rest of the week, the kibbutz would be blanked out and all food, mostly straight out of cans, would be prepared underground. Volunteers would dart out of the shelters between salvoes to milk the cows and feed the chickens. It was the time of the first harvest, and the kibbutz, unable to irrigate, would fall far behind in its work schedule.

Most of the first day's shells fell near the boundary line, but one set, again in a cluster of 14, marched straight up a well-manicured lawn separating two rows of cottages. The potholes ran midway down the lawn, as if some landscape architect had had them dug to receive a new avenue of trees. A bit to the left or to the right and they would have taken out a row of houses.

"Our lucky day," said Ben-Yosef, venturing out with others from the council to inspect the damage.

Would their luck hold?

bine and headed out to the trenches on the eastern perimeter, less than a mile and a half from the Syrian border. The trenches had been dug during the 1948 war, but were deepened and improved since then. With him went Richard Fox, an American Jewish boy from New York City, who had come back to the kibbutz just a few days before to resume his Hebrew studies, after returning briefly to America to see about the opening of a pizza stand he operated summers at Lake George, New York.

Efraim, the Fines' 15-year-old boy, went to the underground communications center to man a telephone. Baruch, a year younger, wanted to help out, too, but his age group was sent down to the shelters. To his dismay and chagrin, teachers were on hand to continue his high school classes. The youngest brother, eight-year-old Ishay, had been in the shelter since the previous evening; now he was playing checkers with his friends and waiting for story hour to begin.

The shelling began about 2:30 P.M. The rounds fell in sets, each consisting of 14

TUESDAY

"TOUGH, GRIM AND CERTAINLY NOT EASY"

■ Now suddenly, it seemed that tiny, out-numbered Israel was bigger than life-size; overnight David had outgrown Goliath. With breathtaking precision, with grim thoroughness, the Israeli war machine ground on through Tuesday. With jet fighter-bombers pounding static enemy positions in the dunes, it completed the noose around the last organized Egyptian resistance in the Sinai. And with napalm and bombs clouding the hills of Jerusalem in smoke and death, it cracked through the desper-ately held lines of the Arab Legion to en-circle the Old City.

For the Egyptian army, ill-disciplined, maintenance-poor, weakened by the isola-tion of 60,000 troops in distant Yemen, Tuesday was an awful day of reckoning. Now the stresses of modern warfare and constant exposure to air attack would pull it apart. For Nasser, Tuesday crashed in all around him like an angry bill collector to settle accounts for one political adven-ture, one bluster, one threat too many.

For Jordan's tough Arab Legion, it was another lesson. Courage and discipline were its forte. But desert-born virtues and British-forged doggedness were not enough to fight a modern war, not enough to pro-tect units from the ravages of air strikes and the brutal shock of quick-moving armor.

For Syria and its long-bloodied border with Israel, it was a day of more artillery fire. From the Golan hills, Syrian guns fired down at Israeli positions in the farms and kibbutzim. And with increasing frequency—

Gaza City falls to the Israelis.

ominous for the Syrians—Israeli jets pummeled the fortified Syrian positions in the heights.

Israeli air power poured it on Arab positions all day, distracted only briefly by isolated, futile missions by remnants of the Arab air forces. Ultimately it destroyed 452 Arab aircraft, 90 percent of them in Monday's surprise attacks.

In the Sinai, the Israeli battle plan that budded Monday morning grew and became clear Tuesday. The westward dash of armored columns along the three major east-west routes moved into high gear. Large chunks of Nasser's army were cut off by encircling Israeli troops, in a series of giant pivots. The Egyptians, who always favored entrenched warfare, were forced by Israeli planes to dig in deeper, making their positions even more static. Constantly, the Israelis spun forces off their main drives to encircle Egyptian fortifications, attacking the eastward-aimed artillery from the west, chewing positions to bits. The Egyptians soon found their artillery largely gone and Israeli armor could now fire almost without answer. What the Egyptians had constructed as lines of defense now became small islands of disorganized opposition, lost in a sea of Israeli troops.

In the north, Brigadier Tal's thrust bypassed pockets of Egyptian resistance around El Arish. Egyptian forces reorganized at nearby El Jiradi along the coast road. In the early morning hours, Israeli armored infantry smashed the hastily-formed Egyptian line and cleared the road for the dash toward El Qantara astride the Suez Canal. Brigadier Tal split off some of his tank forces and sent them southward. They fought a pitched battle with Egyptian tanks for the El Arish airfield, and opened it to Israeli planes by afternoon. Then they continued to plunge southward, linking up with Brigadier Joffe's central drive. Together they smashed Bir Lachfan and its fortifications. Now Joffe committed his reserves, and the refreshed Israeli assault drove on toward Jebel Libni to the southwest along the old road that led from Beersheba in Israel to Ismailiya on the Suez

Canal. Here the combined forces broke through what seemed to be a second Egyptian line of defense, and hurtled onward toward Bir Gifgafa to lock a second escape route to Egypt proper.

In the extreme south, Brigadier Sharon crushed the opposition at Abu Ageila and rushed southward to El Quseima, pursuing the fleeing Egyptians and destroying about 400 tanks with air strikes and artillery. Sharon's pursuit brought his columns to a link-up with the smaller armored brigade that had smashed out of El Kuntilla and was racing toward Mitla Pass, the southernmost exit to the Egyptian homeland. Up until now, the fighting had been what Israeli soldiers called "tough, grim, and certainly not easy." But the break was coming. The Egyptian army, torn from the air and flushed from its best positions, was being pursued on the ground. The war of attrition had begun.

Now, out of Israel came the long vans of resupply. It was a strange-looking army—panel trucks from Tel Aviv businesses, private cars and taxicabs, daubed with mud for camouflage. Tractors from kibbutzim pulled farm carts loaded with ammunition and stores. Dispatch riders scooted up and down columns on motor scooters. Tel Aviv buses, one marked "The Cairo Express," carried troops. Captured and repaired Egyptian trucks and tanks, painted with white stripes to protect them from Israeli planes, were pressed into service. Many citizen-soldiers wore almost any kind of uniform, sport shirts, floppy Australian-style bush hats, bits and pieces of khaki left over from other wars. Some wore beards and skullcaps. Jaffa oranges were passed out as field rations. There were few insignias of rank and little saluting. They spoke German and Polish and Russian and French—the languages of their origins—but took orders in Hebrew and English. But what the Israeli army lacked in military appearance, they made up in courage and elan and training. Israeli reservists who practice tactics at night and sleep during the day in training, kept the columns moving around the clock. They forced the Egyptians from the roads, and the furious sands and rugged mountains of the Sinai did the rest.

The spearheads, moving too fast for ground supply, had a quicker route: the air. Israeli planes air-dropped water and other supplies as temperatures reached 130 degrees Fahrenheit in the afternoon.

By the end of Tuesday, the three-pronged attack of the Israeli columns had reached nearly two-thirds of the way across the Sinai, were close to the three bottlenecks from which they could close off the Sinai to fleeing Egyptians. And the Egyptians, leaving their tanks and trucks behind, were pouring into the desert bound on foot for the same goals—the winding Mitla Pass through the southern mountains, the Bir Gifgafa road between the mountains and impassable dunes in the center, and on the open northern road at El Qantara.

For the Palestinian Liberation Army, besieged in the Gaza Strip, Tuesday was essentially the end of the war. The fighting was bitter. The Israelis reinforced their troops with more tanks and fought a fierce street-by-street battle across Gaza town. Civilians hid in shelters while the tank battle raged in the square. In the center of town, two tanks were burning, one an Israeli Centurion, the other an Egyptian T-54. One Israeli tank came upon the statue of a Palestinian refugee pointing toward Israel, which, the inscription said, was their homeland. The tank demolished it with a single shot. By noon Tuesday, the Israelis held the center of Gaza town, and were salvaging Egyptian vehicles, bending back the license plates to make them unreadable, and driving them off to Israel.

In Jordan's northern hills the war flared to life in the early darkness of Tuesday, and the fighting pace heightened in the hills of Jerusalem to the south. Around the ancient city, the Israeli forces forged their pincers. It was slow going against the stubborn Arab Legion. But backed by around-the-clock air strikes and artillery fire, the Israeli troops kept picking away at Legion positions in the hills surrounding the Old City.

Before the day's first light came, the Is-raeli forces in the north around Jenin fought pitched battles with Arab Legion contingents there. There were heavy losses on both sides. And then up from Jerusalem, the Israelis sent a column swinging northward—tanks in the lead—to begin the huge pincers that ultimately would enclose the Jordanian bulge and extend Israeli dominance to the west bank of the Jordan River.

At 3 A.M. (Israeli time) the Israeli tanks and troops moved against Jenin near the northern border. The Legionnaires clung to their positions, and from the Israeli front lines came word that the Arab Legion anti-tank guns and Patton tanks, well-placed in the hilly region, were taking a toll of Is-raeli armor. Bitter battles ringed Jenin. Jordanian forces called up reserves—60 Patton tanks that had been held at Tubas, 10 miles to the southeast. The Israelis reorganized, fueled up again and rescued equipment lost in the first assault. Then, calling on air strikes and artillery, they hit again at Legion positions. The new attack carried Jenin, and sent the remaining Legion troops into flight. It had been a costly fight for both sides. But the Israeli tank columns kept their momentum. Reinforced by another armored brigade, they met a new concentration of Jordanian tanks at Kabatiya Junction. The Israelis broke through and pushed on toward Tubas on the road to Nablus, harassed by Jordanian tanks again until sundown.

The main northward-bound arm of the Israeli pincers also struck forward early Tuesday, aiming at Ramallah, and the roads that led to the west bank of the Jordan River. They fought an early tank battle at Tel-el-Fol, then Sha'afat on the drive's southern flank, and then Mitvar Hill. But not so easily on Mitvar Hill. In this attack, all hell broke loose over the Israelis. Their tanks and troops withered in Arab fire. Losses were heavy, and the Israelis backed off. Then, regrouped, they hurled themselves again at the hill and finally took it. After that French Hill fell easily, and with the southern flank protected, the main body headed northward to link up with the drive from Jenin. New forces met them at Atrun,

and they sliced up the mountainous course with armored troops entering Ramallah, a summer resort in the mountains, by nightfall. There was little opposition.

Men died in the northern battles, and men died in the south, but the focus of Israeli hearts, and those of Jews around the world, was Jerusalem. And in the old part of that city, the focus in the dark hours of Tuesday morning was on the hills to the north and south and east of the city.

To take the prize of Jerusalem, Colonel Mordechai Gur, commander of a paratroop brigade, worked out a three-pronged attack aimed at sparing the Old City the punishment of air attack and artillery, but finally delivering it into Israeli hands. One force would drive across Mount Scopus and the Mount of Olives and sweep down from the north through St. Stephen's Gate. A second force would push its way through the southern hills from camps in the new City and cross over Mount Zion and the Valley of Hinnon, through the Garden of Gethsemane to St. Stephen's Gate. If needed, a frontal assault would try to penetrate the Jaffa Gate.

Throughout the predawn hours, Gur's paratroopers, backed by a deadly artillery barrage, pushed into the modern, fashionable area northwest of the Old City. Sheltered by darkness, the Israeli troops cut their way through coils of barbed wire entanglements and hit at entrenched Arab Legion positions beyond. The battle rose and fell, from house to house, street by street for some four hours. Casualties were heavy on both sides. Inch by inch, Gur's men took the Sheikh-Jarrah quarter, the modern American colony, The Rockefeller Museum, the police school, and established a corridor to Mount Scopus. The Arab Legion was tenacious, but they were exposed even at night to the Israeli jets blasting away at the searchlight and flare-lit hills. All day Tuesday Jordanian artillery answered back.

In early afternoon, the Jerusalem Brigade attacked Abu Tor, a strategic hill east-southeast of the Old City. Again the Arab Legion fought to the end, and wounded Israeli paratroopers entering Hadassah Hospital in the New City told the nurses over and over of the bravery of the Legion. Finally Abu Tor fell. The Israelis began scouring the area for snipers. Late Tuesday they took positions for the final attack on the Old City itself. Then they rested and waited for dawn. Beyond in the darkness, flickering with the small flashes of rifles, the sacred city waited, too.

■ It was 7:37 A.M. on the banks of the Nile, 37 minutes after midnight on the banks of the Potomac, when Cairo Radio interrupted its martial music for a communiqué from the Supreme Command of the Egyptian armed forces:

". . . It has now become certain that, in a comprehensive manner, the United States and Britain are taking part in the Israeli military aggression as far as the air operations are concerned. It has been fully proved that some of the British and American aircraft carriers are carrying out wide-scale activity in helping Israel.

"As to the Egyptian front, the American and British planes have created an air umbrella over Israel. As regards the Jordanian front, these planes are playing an actual role in the operations against the Jordanian forces, as was shown by the Jordanian radar screens which clearly showed this air activity in support of Israel.

"King Hussein of Jordan early this morning got in touch with President Gamal Abdel Nasser and informed him that he is now confident that British and American aircraft have been playing a serious role in the battle. This confirmed information available from the Egyptian front.

"The king and the president agreed that this serious development should be announced to the entire Arab nation . . ."

Hussein, however, didn't get around to announcing it over Amman Radio until more than four hours later, and then without direct reference to either America or Britain but only "imperialist Western powers" with aircraft carriers in the Mediterranean. Minutes later Amman Radio was back on the air with America's firm denial. Unlike Nasser, whose Cairo Radio repeated the charge over and over, Hussein apparently didn't have much stomach for pushing it.

The charge was false, but not unexpected. Should Egypt go down to defeat after all of Nasser's bluster about "extermination," it would be a far easier blow for his people to accept if they could be made to believe despised little Israel had not done it alone.

Israeli intelligence intercepted what it said was a telephone conversation early Tuesday morning between Nasser and Jordan's Hussein in which they concocted the whole story:

Nasser: "Hello. Will we say the U.S. and England or just the U.S.?"

Hussein: "The U.S. and England."

Nasser: "Does Britain have aircraft carriers?"

Hussein: (Answer unintelligible)

Nasser: "Good. King Hussein will make an announcement and I will make an announcement. Thank you. Do not give up. Yes. Hello, good morning brother. Never mind, be strong. Yes, I hear."

Hussein: "Mr. President, if you have something or any idea at all . . . at any time."

Nasser: "We are fighting with all our strength and we have battles going on on every front all night and if we had any trouble in the fighting it does not matter, we will overcome despite this. God is with us. Will His Majesty make an announcement on the participation of Americans and the British?"

Hussein: (Answer unintelligible.)

Nasser: "By God, I say that I will make an announcement and you will make an announcement and we will see to it that the Syrians will make an announcement that

American and British airplanes are taking part against us from aircraft carriers. We will issue an announcement. We will stress the matter and we will drive the point home."

Hussein: "Good. All right."

Nasser: "Your Majesty, do you agree?"

Hussein: (Answer unintelligible.)

Nasser: "A thousand thanks. Do not give up. We are with you with all our hearts and we are flying our planes over Israel today. Our planes are striking at Israel's airfields since morning."

Hussein: "A thousand thanks. Be well."

The Soviet Union, for its part, wasn't likely to believe the story in the first place. The United States had two aircraft carriers, the *Saratoga* and the *America,* in the Sixth Fleet's 50-vessel force on training exercises in the Mediterranean. Soviet warships had been shadowing the fleet for at least a week and knew the carriers' every move.

Some diplomats viewed Nasser's charge of American intervention as an implied appeal to the Soviets for help. If that were the case, it did not seem to affect negotiations between the United States and Russia to bring about a cease-fire.

There were a series of hot-line exchanges between Washington and Moscow. President Johnson, who had awakened for the second day at 4:30 A.M., seemed relaxed as he worked at his desk through the morning. In Moscow, Premier Kosygin met with the Egyptian ambassador, and the British ambassador paid a call on the Soviet deputy foreign minister. And at the United Nations, where all the parleying eventually would focus, U.S. Ambassador Arthur Goldberg and Soviet Ambassador Nikolai Fedorenko met twice in the morning, twice again in the afternoon. They were determined to present a cease-fire resolution to the Security Council. They only question was the terms.

Reports from the battlefront of Israeli successes could only strengthen Goldberg's bargaining position. Moreover, it was an open secret that Jordan was putting out guarded pleas for the United States to press for a quick end to the agony. By now Jor-

dan's miniscule air force was virtually wiped out and its vaunted Arab Legion was being pummeled from the air. It was a sad irony. For years its 31-year-old ruler, Hussein, had walked a tightrope between East and West. Because of his friendship with the West he had suffered the external slings of his Arab brethren. And within his kingdom, 600,000 Palestinian refugees, more than half the Arabs displaced by the creation of the state of Israel, were a continual source of internal unrest. Hussein wanted the killing to end. Quickly.

At 4:27 P.M. Ambassador Goldberg phoned the White House. He told the President that he and Fedorenko had agreed on a cease-fire resolution. He told him the terms. Fedorenko would drop the Russian demand for withdrawal of troops as a condition for a cease-fire; he would present it later as a separate question. President Johnson summoned his press secretary, George Christian. Together they drafted a "reaction" statement which the President would read over television as soon as the Security Council passed the resolution.

That came two and a half hours later. Security Council President Tabor, fatigued but obviously relieved, called the Council into session and read the resolution. The vote was unanimous. The resolution said:

"The Security Council

"Noting the oral report of the Secretary-General in this situation,

"Having heard the statements made in the Council,

"Concerned at the outbreak of fighting and with the menacing situation in the Near East,

"1. Calls upon the governments concerned as a first step to take forthwith all measures for an immediate cease-fire and for a cessation of all military activities in the area.

"2. Requests the Secretary-General to keep the Council promptly and currently informed on the situation."

It was a beginning. As word of the Council's action flashed around the globe Gold-

From the sky, supplies during the push south in Sinai.

An Israeli paratroop commander.

berg, the silver-haired American ambassador, stepped to the podium. There were some loose ends.

There have been reports, said Ambassador Goldberg, that United States aircraft have intervened in the war on Israel's behalf. That is erroneous, he said. The United States, he said, was prepared to invite United Nations investigators aboard carriers in the Mediterranean to examine official logs and question air crews. "And in the meantime," he said, "I ask any government interested in peace to see to it that these false and inflammatory charges are given no further credence by any source within its control."

Next on the podium was Israeli Foreign Minister Abba Eban. He had arrived in New York only hours before.

"I have just come from Jerusalem," he said, "to tell the Security Council that Israel, by her independent effort and sacrifice, has passed from serious danger to successful resistance." In a low-keyed voice, Eban reviewed Israel's woes over the years, apologized lightly for having had to arouse the

UN chairman "at a most uncongenial hour of the night," and outlined certain principles upon which he said "the situation to be constructed after the cease-fire must depend.

"The first of these principles surely must be the acceptance of Israel's statehood and the total elimination of the fiction of her nonexistence. It would seem to me that after 3,000 years the time has arrived to accept Israel's nationhood as a fact.

"Here is the only state in the international community which has the same territory, speaks the same language, and upholds the same faith as it did 3,000 years ago.

"There is an intellectual tragedy in the failure of Arab leaders to come to grips, however reluctantly, with the depth and authenticity of Israel's roots in the light of the history of the spiritual experience and the culture of the Middle East."

Eban spoke of the withdrawal of the UN force from Egypt's border with a telling metaphor.

"People in our country and in many countries ask: what is the use of a United Nations presence if it is in effect an umbrella which is taken away as soon as it begins to rain?"

In conclusion, he said, the war could have a beneficial result if those who brought it on "would ask themselves what the results and benefits have been as they look around them at the arena of battle, at the wreckage of planes and tanks, at the collapse of intoxicated hopes. Might not an Egyptian ruler ponder whether anything was achieved by that disruption? What has it brought but strife, conflict with other powerful interests and a stern criticism of progressive men throughout the world?"

"I think," he said, "that Israel has proved her steadfastness and vigor in recent days. She is now willing to demonstrate her instinct for peace."

The speech was moving. There was applause. Next on the podium was George J. Tomen, the representative from Syria. His speech was short. Mr. Eban, he said, had avoided the main issue: the Palestinian refugees.

"Until and unless the Arab people of

The Star of David flies from an Arab minaret.

Palestine are recognized by Israel and by the Israeli people themselves as being the third party to the dispute, we will continue . . . to deal only with palliatives and not with the solution of the problem."

"Mr. President," he continued, "at this juncture of the Middle East crisis, the delegation of the Syrian Arab Republic wishes to place on record that the governments of the United States and of Great Britain, by their actions in collusion with the Israeli aggressors, have proved beyond any doubt to be the bitter enemies of the Arab nations."

The time for set rhetoric was over. It was time again for debate. Soviet Ambassador Fedorenko told the Council it was its duty now to adopt another resolution, this one calling for the "immediate and unconditional withdrawal" of Israeli forces. But the Council had done enough for one day. It adjourned.

In .Washington, President Johnson delivered his prepared statement praising the Security Council's action. By then he had received word that Egypt and a brace of other Arab nations had severed diplomatic relations with the United States.

But diplomatic relations can be restored. Lives can't. Who would stop the killing?

Cairo Radio announced the break in diplomatic relations at 5 P.M. Moments later, Richard Nolte, the U.S. Ambassador-designate to Cairo, was summoned to the Egyptian Foreign Ministry to receive the official announcement. It came from Under-secretary Ahmed el Fekky.

Three hours earlier Ambassador Nolte had been in the office of Egyptian Foreign Minister Mahmoud Riad trying to convince Riad that if Egypt persisted in its false claim of U.S. intervention in the war it was going to be most harmful to American-Egyptian relations. Nolte said Riad appeared genuinely to believe the claim.

Meeting with El Fekky, Nolte expressed regret that Egypt had determined to break relations on the basis of erroneous information. El Fekky seemed to Nolte to look a bit sheepish.

Cairo Radio followed its announcement of the diplomatic rupture with a steady stream of anti-American propaganda. Throughout the afternoon and evening the city was under almost continuous air raid alert.

From the terrace outside The Associated Press office, Cairo Correspondent Garven Hudgins was watching an air raid in the distance when he received a telephone call from Colonel Abdel Zaki of Egyptian Military Intelligence. Hudgins, said the Colonel, would have to leave Egypt immediately. How? asked Hudgins, pointing out that no air traffic was moving in or out of Cairo and the situation in Alexandria was unclear.

Hours later an Egyptian army officer came to The Associated Press bureau and placed Hudgins under arrest. The departing American newsman shook hands all around with his Egyptian colleagues, wished them well, hoped his arrest would not bring them difficulties. They wished him well.

Hudgins was taken to the Nile Hotel, a small building with only one entrance. Other American citizens arrived—newsmen, tourists, teachers, missionaries. Soon a platoon of scruffy soldiers carrying shields and long riot poles pulled up in a truck with a Pepsi-Cola sign on the side and stationed themselves around the hotel.

◼ Midnight, the coming of the second day. Still the bombs fell on the Arab Legionnaires of Major Mohammed Ibn Jamil. From the intensity of the artillery and bombing around the Ambassador Hotel, the major was sure the Israelis would try to break through there.

Then, in the dark of early morning, the jets were gone. There was a new sound: the rasp of steel treads on pavement and the deep grumbling of diesel engines. Tanks.

About 1:30 A.M. a brigade of Israeli tanks drove through the Jordanian line near the hotel and turned south along the paved road bordering no-man's-land. Israeli troops also moved up in armored personnel carriers. In 1948 they had come in cars and makeshift armored cars. Not now.

To the north, Jordanian tanks tangled with Israeli armor. "We definitely outfought them," a fellow officer of Major Jamil would say later. "Our men were definitely better trained and disciplined. In the tank battles they shot at our tanks with regular high explosive shells, whereas we fired armor-piercing shells at them. They were probably confused."

"Yes, yes, they were definitely confused," another Legionnaire would say. "It is well known that the Jews are cowards."

But by 2 A.M. someone told Major Jamil the forward Jordanian posts had been overrun. He thought the men were paratroops who had been landed by helicopter. But it was too dark to be certain. Anyway, they were there. It was time to attack, orders or not.

"Fix bayonets," Major Jamil ordered. Then, as his warrior ancestors had done for ages past, he led his men into battle.

Face to face, hand to hand, Arab battled Jew. The only light now came from the muzzle blasts of the automatic weapons and rifles. Some time around 3 A.M. an Israeli machine gunner seeking to reconquer his Holy City fired towards Major Mohammed Ibn Jamil seeking to defend one of his. The major fell.

■ The bell on Jerusalem's Y.M.C.A. tower chimed once, a crystal soprano note that floated free in the crisp, cool night.

One A.M.

The paratroopers moved out under the stars. A thin scimitar of a moon—the Turk's moon, as Captain Matan Goor had called it—had set behind the Judean hills, and the wind was beginning to rise, redolent with the acrid odor of cordite and jet fuel. Their passage out of the New City toward Mount Scopus and the encirclement of the Old City was noisy and relatively uneventful. Artillery batteries and mortar crews from both sides banged away back and forth across those ancient hills, bathed in the eerie glow of giant searchlights, and every now and then Israeli jets screamed down on

A recoilless rifle blasts Syrian positions on Israel's northern front.

Arab Legionnaires tenaciously dug into the catacombs that were the burial places for the kings of Judea.

Hugging the tree line, Goor's men moved along a black ribbon of highway. They picked their way past russet-painted armored cars with long-dead funeral wreaths across their hoods, stark memorials to convoys that battled through Arab ambush and booby traps to bring supplies to the starving city during the 1948 siege. Farther on, there were newer memorials to the new war, flaming sacrifices of bombed-out tanks and burning trucks and half-tracks. In the crevices of the terraced hills, out of range of the probing searchlights, the sheen of starlight fell softly on the random outcroppings of other ages, other endeavors:

the ghostly ruins of a Roman aqueduct, a grove of silver-leafed olive trees, the squat cupola of a 12th-century Crusader church, the sudden needle thrust of a minaret out of a drab Arab village, a dead donkey still in the traces of its toppled cart, the red slate roof and gleaming white facade of an American-style gasoline station, a slant-roofed bus shelter with a large advertisement pushing the virtues of El Al Airlines. Then, farther still, across the snipped strands of barbed wire that only minutes ago constituted the border, another slant-roofed bus shelter, nearly battered down, but with its large advertisement still intact pushing the merits of Syrian Airways.

From there on out, there was fighting such as none of the veterans on either side,

The grisly toll in Sinai.

paratroopers or Legionnaires, had ever experienced before. From trench to trench, bunker to bunker, up over the terraced hills, down into the dark crevices of bleak valleys, the bloody battle surged amid a shrill cacophony of machine guns, recoilless rifles, mortar fire and artillery barrage. Taking heavy losses, so that sometimes only four or five were still together in the same platoon, the Israelis moved doggedly forward on the heavily-entrenched Arab Legionnaires. The Legionnaires fell back reluctantly, gallantly, in the best traditions of Lawrence of Arabia and Glubb Pasha, so that sometimes their zeal and tenacity left 30 Jordanian bodies in a ditch, sprawled beside a still-smoking 50-caliber machine gun with its empty cartridge belt hanging out like a leering tongue.

Dawn comes swift and early in the Middle East. 4:37 Israeli time. 5:37 Arab time. By first light, the northern prong had fought its way past the Mandelbaum Gate, named for that unfortunate doctor whose house was neatly cut in half by the 1948 Armistice Line. It had stormed and taken Sheikh Jarrah, the strongly defended Jordanian Police Training School that had refused to fall in the War of Independence. Through bitterly contested, mine-infested open fields, fighting from one fence line to the next, the column moved remorselessly over the rim of Mount Scopus and the east shoulder of the Mount of Olives down into the Valley of Jehoshaphat, the deep cleft that separates the Old City from the surrounding hills with their skyline of modern hotels, hospitals and museums. Coming out into a road once more, Goor's unit fell back to let a tank column roll by, then moved into a section of well-kept Jordanian homes known as the American colony. Day broke on a scene of brutal battle, cellar to cellar, rooftop to rooftop, down deserted streets echoing with the whine of sniper fire, in and out of the houses, across courtyards, into the lobbies of hotels and *pensions,* where the literature on the desk counters offered pilgrimages to the holy places.

In the lulls between the fighting, engineers crawled out with their mine detectors. Tanks pushed burning trucks and buses out of the way, often rolling over them and flattening them like discarded beer cans, so the half-tracks and armored personnel carriers could get in position for the assault on the walled Old City, still a vision, a whole day's fighting away in the distance. Jordanian Patton tanks, arrayed in a defensive pattern along the connecting road to the heights on which stood the Augusta Victoria Hospital, belched fire and devastation in the already blackened streets of the American colony.

At 10:15 A.M. Captain Goor walked into the lobby of the Ambassador Hotel, a shambles of broken glass and smashed chandeliers, and flopped down into a Romanesque-type lobby chair. It was high-backed and low-armed, so that he sat upright like one of Caesar's tribunes in a judicial pose, attuned to the people's woes. There were woes aplenty. He heard for the first time of friends who had died in the fighting, friends of 16 and 17 years. The captain was tired—it was the first rest he had taken since the bell on the Y.M.C.A. tolled their fate—and he felt depressed, as only war and death can depress a man. The executive officer was dead. So was the radioman. So was Mordy, the sergeant who called Goor's wife in Pardess Hana two days before and told her not to worry, that everything would be all right.

Back in Pardess Hana, Goor's wife, Simcha, was looking out into the orange grove they had planted behind the house. Ahmad Ben Essa, their Arab handyman, had not reported to work today. It was the second day of the war. He was afraid. Even with the war news coming in over the radio from Kol Yisrael's half-hourly broadcasts, Simcha felt sorry for him. They had all gotten along so well together. He was a hard worker and careful about the irrigation equipment.

Street by street, the fighting continued in the American colony of Jerusalem. At 11:30 A.M. Captain Goor was entering the main floor of the Rockefeller Museum of Antiquity, one of the world's great treasure troves of learning, just as Arab Legionnaires were fleeing out the back door and into the garden. On the terrazzo floor, the captain spread out some maps of old Jerusalem, and the other officers gathered around, hunkering down in an intense circle, presided over by gaunt skeletons leering down from the glass exhibition cases. A bas-relief map of the Old City on the wall behind them caught the captain's eye. It was more like a scale model, and to his surprise and satisfaction its detail was more helpful and revealing than any of his military maps. The planning conference immediately arrayed itself around the museum map. At one point in the session, Goor looked about him and beheld, amid the rubble of the fighting, diorama displays of ancient cave-dwelling civilizations in exquisite detail, jars and urns from the burial mounds of lost and forgotten kingdoms, the mummies and robes and regalia of vanished emperors and vanquished queens. He thought it was a strange place in which to fight a war.

But still better maps would be needed for the final thrust into the Old City, maps that spelled out in unmistakable detail the location of the shrines and mosques and holy places, so they could be spared. With four others, Captain Goor went back to new Jerusalem to request some more maps from Brigade Forward, the combat headquarters that had moved up with the fighting.

Their jeep entered Israeli Jerusalem through the cobblestoned lanes and narrow passageways of Mea Shearim, the severely Orthodox section of the city where Eastern Jews had faithfully recreated the Polish ghettos and Russian *shtetels* of a past they refused to relinquish. Captain Goor and his intelligence team were among the first to return to the city from the fighting, and they passed down a gauntlet of uncontrolled emotions. Old men with beards and young boys in *peytoth,* the long side curls that bespoke the biblical injunction against shaving, stood in the streets, unabashedly weeping, calling out prayers in Yiddish. Although it was Tuesday, some were dressed in their Sabbath best, out of respect for what they called "the Holy War," wearing the black kaftans (long overcoats) and furbrimmed round hats echoing the costumes of long-dead Polish noblemen.

The jeep passed under a streamer, stretched from a building: "Daughters of Israel, Observe Modesty In These Streets!"—a warning to the godless tourists, and the captain mused upon the way war had of drawing together the dissident factions in the tiny country. On other days, holy days in particular, they might be stoned and spat upon for roaring through the Orthodox quarter at breakneck speed. Now the people were weeping and cheering and calling out "God be with you!"

The captain picked up the maps in the busy headquarters enclave and headed back to his unit. Behind him on his right, as he once more drove out of the New City, was Mount Zion, sacred to Jews as the burial place of King David, whose city this was; sacred to Christians as the traditional location of the Upper Room, the cénacle, where

Egyptian officers under guard.

Christ spent Passover with His apostles, the Last Supper. Crowning the mount was the Church of the Dormition, where Mary went to sleep, roofless now, its leaden dome burned away by a Jordanian shell, so that the rafters stood out in startlingly modern geodesic design.

The driver gunned the jeep past a lumbering file of tanks, into a deep defile in the Judean hills, so that they passed beneath the towering hospice of Notre Dame de France, lit up by the afternoon sun and silhouetted by occasional cascades of napalm falling in the hills beyond. The road dipped down again and swung past the Rivoli Hotel in a direct line toward the Old City. Directly in front of them now were the rose-gray crenelated walls and the narrow lane leading up to the St. Stephen's Gate or, as the Jews called it, the Lions' Gate, because of the rampant lions of Judah high up above its arched entranceway. Here at last was the resting place for the hopes and dreams of all Jewish leaders from David the King to David Ben-Gurion, the lodestone of Jewish yearning the world over, so that all synagogues everywhere were built with their Sacred Arks pointing in the direction where the great Temple of Solomon had stood.

A Jordanian bus was burning in the stone street leading up to the massive St. Stephen's Gate, the black smoke curling up in a lazy plume out across the highway and drifting in darkish wisps across the Garden of Gethsemane where Jesus wept in His last agony before the betrayal. Just inside the gate and to the left, its great golden dome glittering in the sunlight and afternoon shadows already making intriguing arabesques on its

97

blue and white mosaic walls, was the Mosque of the Dome of the Rock, where the Prophet Mohammed leaped to heaven on his white horse. Directly ahead were the winding streets of the Via Dolorosa, where Christ carried His cross up to the Hill of the Skull. For Captain Goor and his companions in the jeep there was only one sight that interested and thrilled them—the few bold bare stones of the Wailing Wall barely visible above the drab collection of Arab shacks and bazaars that began where the great courtyard of the mosque ended.

They were at *Ir Hakodish*, the Holy Place, but like Moses and the Promised Land, they were denied entrance.

A 30-caliber machine gun chattered in a sweeping arc from inside the shadowy recesses of the St. Stephen's Gate. Goor and his comrades leaped out of the jeep. The curtain of fire made a devastating pass over a column of paratroopers moving along the edge of the road. Men were falling all around him, but of those who had been in the jeep only Goor was hit. He tumbled forward with a stabbing pain in his right leg. The bullet had gone through the bone below the knee. The captain lay in the road in front of the Rivoli Hotel. He took a combat compress from his cartridge belt but he

couldn't reach down to the wound. The machine gun at the Gate pivoted back to begin another sweeping arc. A medic named Chico ran out and threw himself on top of the captain. The medic dragged him into an abandoned house and applied a tourniquet. Even then the captain knew that Chico, whoever he was, had saved his life. He never had a chance to thank him because the little medic had dashed outside again to drag in other casualties. It was 3 P.M. when Captain Goor was brought into the building. There were other wounded lying about the room. He could hear them moaning and breathing heavily. The valley beneath Mount Scopus and the Mount of Olives was exploding in flames and smoke now, and there was no chance to get a helicopter in to take out the wounded. The Jordanians were laying down a mortar barrage from the heights around Augusta Victoria, and an Israeli Super Sherman tank was in the street where the bus was burning outside the St. Stephen's Gate, its turret revolving in furious salvos of smoke and flame.

By 7:30 P.M., the sun had disappeared behind the citadel Tower of David and mauve shadows were folding into pastel-tinted hills, empty of the familiar necklace of

Israeli citizen-soldiers pause in Sinai. A Nasser portrait is one fighter's prize.

streetlights now that war had invoked a full blackout on Jerusalem, old and new, save for the searching sweep of the spotlights.

Dusk is as fleeting as dawn in the Middle East, and in 20 minutes it was dark. There was a sudden lull in the fighting around the Rivoli Hotel, except for the occasional bark of a bazooka, licking out a tongue of flame from a vantage point atop the dun-colored Herodian stones somewhere in the vicinity of the St. Stephen's Gate. Even that died in a few minutes, and the medics took advantage of the abrupt break in the fighting to carry Captain Goor out of the house and place him gently on a board across the back seat of a jeep. Suddenly machine-gun fire erupted to the left. The volley ripped into the body of the jeep, cutting down two of the soldiers who had helped carry Goor out of the house. The captain, horizontal on his pallet across the back seat, thought this surely was his final chapter. When the gun finally stopped chattering, after what seemed an agony of waiting and wondering, two more medics ventured forth, lifted the captain from the back of the jeep and carried him a quarter of a mile on a stretcher to a station wagon ambulance waiting in a quieter side street.

Through it all, Captain Goor never lost consciousness. He knew he had been taken to Hadassah Hospital, the marvellous modern medical complex built by the contributions of American Jewish women. Lying on his back, staring at the eggshell fretwork of the overhead fluorescent lights, he could hear the soft hollow echo of nurses' footsteps, moving determinedly, efficiently among the long lines of wounded, some of whom were on stretchers out in the corridors, waiting for attention. He saw the doctors in a circle around his bed, then heard them move off, whispering.

Fortunately, they had moved too far out of his hearing range for him to know the nature of their professional discussion. They were trying to decide, in hurried consultation, whether it would be necessary to amputate his leg. Since no surgeon was available at the moment, the decision was put off until morning.

A nurse came to give the captain a sleeping pill. But he had already dozed off, without knowing that old Jerusalem was still in Jordanian hands.

The final assault, like the doctors' decision, had been put off until morning.

In the narrow streets of the Mea Shearim, the strictly observant Russian and Polish Jews were filing into the synagogue, now darkened and without menorah lamps because of the blackout restrictions.

They prayed together in the ancient language of the *Yeshivot,* the Talmudic schools: "Weep not for Jerusalem . . ."

■ At 4 P.M. the beleaguered Egyptian force at El Kuntilla received the urgent order. Retreat. To Corporal Kamal Mahrouss, proud, professional Egyptian infantryman, it was a moment of personal humiliation. Still, he supposed the decision was inevitable.

The attack on the second day had started in the morning. Israeli planes, alone in the sky, struck with devastating bomb attacks; then Israeli tanks rumbled in from the east. The Israelis were unrelenting, and without air cover Corporal Mahrouss and the others felt helpless.

By 5 P.M. his unit had destroyed what little the enemy had missed, blowing up heavy equipment, dismembering big guns and burying the parts in the sand. Corporal Mahrouss scrambled into a truck. Soon a column of trucks was snaking northwest across the desert toward Ismailiya on the opposite side of the Sinai Peninsula.

Darkness came, but the attacking Israelis pressed the chase. Searchlights pierced the desert night, picked up the fleeing Egyptian column, and tanks opened up with devastating cannon fire. Ahead, another Egyptian column was stalled on the road. It reported bad news. Two Israeli tanks were ahead, blocking the retreat. Now tank fire pounded them from the front and the rear and the retreating Egyptians fled into the desert night in utter disarray, in trucks, on foot, any way they could move. They scattered in the wilderness.

WEDNESDAY

"IF I FORGET THEE, O JERUSALEM . . ."

■ On Wednesday, the Jews came home.

Dawn began to clear the dark of the crooked streets of old Jerusalem and with it came the artillery. It struck at the Jordanian Arab Legion on the Mount of Olives, where Christ had predicted the destruction of Jerusalem and ascended into Heaven, and at Gethsemane, where He prayed after the Last Supper.

The Jordanians still held the city although on Tuesday Israeli soldiers had begun to squeeze a pincer from the hills to the north and the south. In the light of the new day they could see Mount Scopus where the Roman, Titus, had camped before he took the city in 70 A.D. On its summit were the huge old Hadassah Hospital and the Hebrew University, abandoned since 1948. Every week since then a convoy of trucks, boarded so that the passengers could only see the road ahead of them, had carried Israeli police up to the school and the hospital. Every week, by Jordanian agreement, trucks had returned off-duty police back through the Mandelbaum Gate back into Israel.

This day the Israelis came to stay.

At 8:30 A.M. paratroopers dropped on Augusta Victoria near Mount Scopus. Tanks and infantrymen completed the encirclement of the Old City and Israeli soldiers fought through the gates into the city itself, much as David had 3,000 years before. The day had already counted its first dead. They were carried back with handkerchiefs over their faces to separate them from the wounded.

Mordechai Gur, commander of the para-

troop brigade, looked down at the objective of his battle plan, old Jerusalem, its silver cupolas gleaming in the valley below. His battalions advanced before a rolling artillery barrage. All tanks and recoilless guns opened fire from the St. Stephen's Wall northward, but with orders not to direct a single round at any of the holy places. The old Herodian walls quaked, and the massive stones on the embrasures seemed to do a little dance every time a round crashed home. The walls were under constant plastering now. Gur jumped aboard a half-track and ordered the driver to get going. He saw the needle on the speedometer swing around to 55 miles an hour.

They swerved out of line, passing two tanks firing away with everything they had. They rolled past the burnt-out Jordanian bus up the narrow lane to the St. Stephen's Gate. The gate was partially open. Gur expected to find Legionnaires astride the walls, but they had fallen back. On the top of the gate he saw abandoned bazookas and unfired shells.

They crashed through the gate, rumbling up over the stones that had toppled from the wall. They roared through the second gate, swerving past a motorcycle blocking the main road. Gur wondered quickly if the impromptu detour led to a minefield. It didn't. On they raced toward the precious Wailing Wall.

Israeli soldiers fought down the narrow streets, along the drainage ditches bridged by gravestones from the Jewish cemetery on Mount Zion. A platoon assaulted the Dung

From the hills, Israelis swept into the sacred city.

101

Gate (so named because in years past sewage had been dumped there) and was blocked by Jordanian machine guns. The crouched soldiers could see the Dome of the Rock, a holy shrine of Islam, only feet from the cherished stones that remained of Solomon's Temple—the Wailing Wall.

An Arab dashed out of a doorway, his hands in the air. Several guns fired. He fell, in bloody tatters. An old Jordanian and his son came out and surrendered. They were taken prisoner. Others surrendered. They were Jordanian soldiers who had changed to civilian dress. The Israelis mocked them.

Israeli tanks from the Jordanian side of the city rolled through St. Stephen's Gate in the east of the Old City. To their right was a sign saying that the Virgin Mary had been born there. Israeli foot soldiers fanned out towards the Wailing Wall. Jordanian machine gunners shot at them from the gate-house protecting the Dome of the Rock. Arab gunners sent mortar shells sliding along the ancient paving stones towards the Israeli foe. This stopped the first assault. Before another could begin, the Jordanians surrendered the position. The mosque was undamaged except for a broken glass door.

Israeli tanks moved to other parts of the Old City. An Arab officer crashed his white Volkswagen into a tank in a suicide attack. He died. A tread of the tank was slightly damaged.

An Arab half-track, truck and Land Rover mounted with a cannon rounded a corner and met Israeli tanks face to face. The tanks fired, setting the Land Rover and truck on fire. The half-track squeezed past the tanks and sped towards the embassy quarter. The tank turrets turned like eyes at a tennis match and their cannon smashed the fleeing half-track.

Shellfire badly damaged the church of

Israeli soldiers approach Hebron, south of Jerusalem.

102

St. Anne, built by the Crusaders 800 years before. There were holes in the stone roof and two unexploded shells lay in front of the altar. But the golden dome of the Dome of the Rock was undamaged. The Jews had taken pains not to damage the shrines of the three faiths that had left Jerusalem an eternal cockpit.

At 9:10 Israeli tanks and busses were seen carrying infantrymen towards Mount Scopus. Foot soldiers walked up the bare slopes. A mine or a shell occasionally exploded among them in a billow of brown earth. They kept on. Israeli jets, which had been at work earlier, attacked behind the Mount of Olives. A cloud of black smoke from a burning supply dump darkened the valley. By 10:15 ambulances were driving up Mount Scopus. Lorries carrying soldiers were coming down. They had other places to fight. Mount Scopus had been taken.

By midmorning Arab resistance in the Old City was broken. Jordanians lined the cobbled streets, arms in the air. Israeli soldiers checked identity papers. Those suspected of being soldiers were tightly bound and led away. They were now prisoners in their home.

Gur's speeding half-track pulled up short at the Dome of the Rock. The firing had stopped. Gur figured that it would.

Officials of the Old City recognized him, came forward and announced that the Jordanians had unanimously decided to cease all opposition there to prevent further bloodshed. But, the officials said, they couldn't be responsible "for all kinds of bandits" in the streets and narrow alleys. There were brief skirmishes atop the battered walls, but the real battle was over. One battalion straddled the Nablus Gate. Another held the corner of the walls facing the Yemin Moshe quarter. The third faced Mount Zion from the vicinity of the Dung Gate. It was 10 A.M.

Already, weeping Jews, citizen-soldiers, were making their first pilgrimage to the Wailing Wall. They stood and prayed, they knelt and prayed, they caressed and kissed the stones, their faces drawn with the emotions of 2,000 years of flight and persecu-

tion. Above the heads of the soldiers, helmets in their hands, the Wall seemed again a temple, small green plants clinging to its ancient crevices as Jews had clung to the hope of returning here.

"We have taken the city of God," said General Shlomo Goren, Chief Rabbi of the armed forces. "We are entering the messianic era for Jewish people."

Despite sniper fire, the squat rabbi, clad in a paratrooper's gear and decorated with battle ribbons from the wars of 1948 and 1956, stood with Torah in hand, the same blue-sheathed Torah he had carried in previous wars. He vowed:

"I promise to the Christian world that we are responsible for and will take care of the holy places of all religions here. For all people, I promise them, we will take care."

There is no holier place for the Jew than the Wall. Hundreds now stood before the age-old stones, dampening them with their tears as the angels are reputed to have done when Titus destroyed the Second Temple.

"We have waited 1,897 years for this moment," cried a paratrooper, beating his campaign hat in the dust. "Think of it: 1,897 years. Now they will never take it from us. Never!"

Tradition clings like moss to the old stones. Some say that the Wall's foundation rests on seven stones laid each in their time by Adam, Abraham, Isaac, Jacob, Joseph, David and Solomon. Some say that when Solomon first set about building the first temple, he allotted the work among all the people. But the wealthier classes hired others to do their work so that the construction of the west wall eventually fell to the poorest of the poor. For this reason the Shekina, the Divine Presence, gave a special blessing to the west wall and promised its protection would never be removed.

Titus demolished the other three walls in 70 A.D. But the first Roman general who approached the west wall fell dead, tradition says. Titus himself then raised a sledge to smite the wall but his right hand withered. At that moment six angels sat atop the wall weeping and their tears, seeping between the stones, hardened into a cement

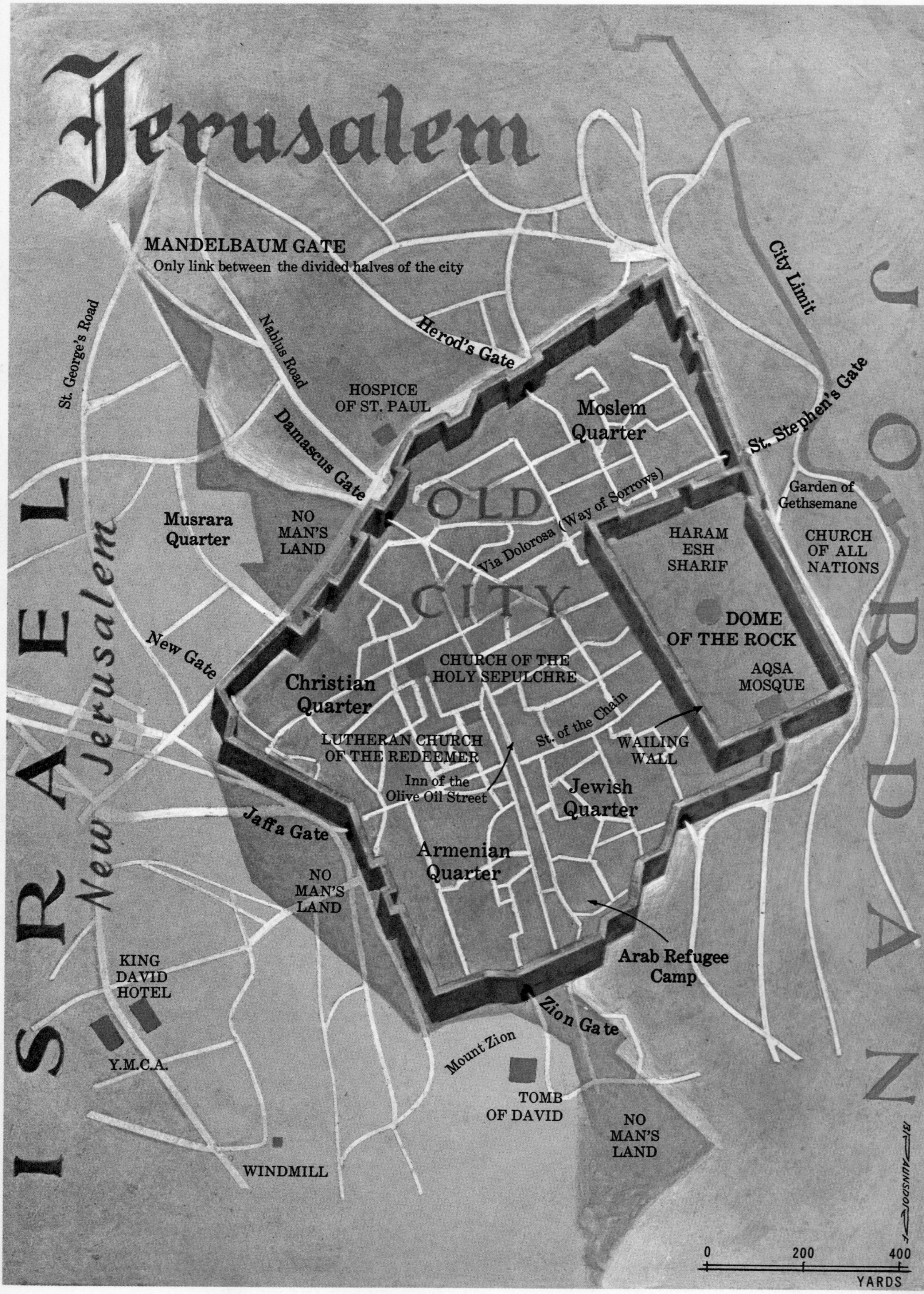

Jerusalem

New Jerusalem

St. George's Road

Nablus Road

MANDELBAUM GATE
Only link between the divided halves of the city

Herod's Gate

City Limit

HOSPICE
OF ST. PAUL

Moslem
Quarter

St. Stephen's Gate

Damascus Gate

OLD

Garden of
Gethsemane

Musrara
Quarter

NO
MAN'S
LAND

Via Dolorosa (Way of Sorrows)

HARAM
ESH
SHARIF

CHURCH
OF ALL
NATIONS

CITY

New Gate

DOME
OF THE ROCK

Christian
Quarter

CHURCH OF THE
HOLY SEPULCHRE

AQSA
MOSQUE

LUTHERAN CHURCH
OF THE REDEEMER

St. of the Chain

WAILING
WALL

Inn of the
Olive Oil Street

Jewish
Quarter

Jaffa Gate

Armenian
Quarter

NO
MAN'S
LAND

Arab Refugee
Camp

KING
DAVID
HOTEL

Y.M.C.A.

Zion Gate

Mount Zion

TOMB
OF DAVID

NO
MAN'S
LAND

WINDMILL

J O R D A N

0   200   400
YARDS

that has bound the rock ever since. One of the lesser Roman officers finally convinced Titus that by leaving one wall intact, history would be able to better gauge the dimension of his great victory. Impressed and flattered, Titus accepted the solution but ordered the officer to jump off the wall for disobeying his orders to destroy it.

Now another leader stood before the wall. "We have returned to the holiest of our holy places, never to depart from it again," said Moshe Dayan.

Mrs. Yohanan Beham, "not at all religious", nonetheless made her way to the Wall and, by tradition, wrote on a scrap of paper the names of her children and stuffed it into a crevice between the stones. (She didn't know then that one of her children, a paratrooper, had been killed in battle.) Others had to be told the way to the Wall. They had never been there before.

One of the first civilians to enter the Old City was combat artist Jossi Stern. To him the streets seemed unchanged since he had been there last, 20 years before. The same Arab merchants, smiling and sleepy, stood in the doorways of the same shops along the Via Dolorosa, waiting for business to resume and the tourists to return. Veiled Arab woman hurried along the same cobblestones balancing huge stone casks on their heads.

Mordechai Gur looked proudly at his dirt-smeared, dog-tired men, racing toward the Wailing Wall in surges of tears and jubilation. They were, a few days ago, shopkeepers, clerks, farmers, schoolteachers, most of them overage, even overweight for such grueling street-to-street fighting.

"The pick of the best," he said to an aide.

It had cost him 96 lives to storm the Old City Crusader-style, through the gates and breeches torn open in the walls, instead of flattening the Old City in the manner of modern warfare. The radiant faces of paratroopers approaching the Western Wall made it all seem worthwhile. Inside the Mosque of Omar they found an arsenal of mortars and machine-gun ammunition.

But death had not done. A sniper's bullet killed a soldier praying at the base of

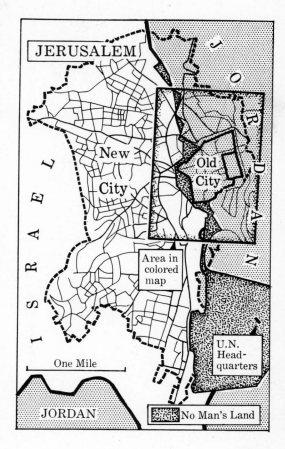

the Wall. Gunfire continued into the night. Two Israeli soldiers running through the darkness to reach the Wall were cut down accidentally by fellow troopers. Israeli soldiers were told to stop singing lest snipers determine their position. But their only fear would be snipers.

With the fall of old Jerusalem, the fate of the Jordanian bulge was sealed. The Israeli drives from Jenin in the north and Ramallah in the south closed a pincers over the bulge and pushed back the tattered Arab Legion to the east bank of the Jordan River. The city of Nablus, pounded from the air for almost a day, fell with little opposition.

At 10 P.M. Jordan and Israel agreed to a cease-fire. For 15,000 Jordanian soldiers, the *jihad* was over. They were dead.

In the Sinai too, Wednesday was a day of triumph for Israel. Tanks and armor closed off the escape routes over the Suez Canal, and stranded Nasser's Sinai Army without hope of reinforcement or supply, and almost without hope.

Brigadier Tal's coastal forces reached Romani, only 20 miles from the Canal. The middle column reached Bir Gifgafa by 11 A.M., fencing with Egyptian tanks fighting a rear-guard maneuver. At Bir Gifgafa, Israeli tanks were let loose to close what seemed a likely Egyptian escape route. An Egyptian force came up from the southwest, trying to break through the Israeli blockade with the support of husbanded Egyptian jets. Israeli tanks repulsed them, and took the counteroffensive. In the battle they destroyed an entire Egyptian mechanized brigade.

Wednesday night, another Egyptian force of some 60 tanks tried to break through from the Suez Canal side to open the way again for the retreating Sinai force. For more than two hours a light brigade of Israeli tanks held them off despite casualties until reinforcements arrived. Then the entire command pushed on slowly toward the Canal against delaying tactics by Egyptian tanks and aircraft.

The columns split and encircled still more Egyptian troops to the north and south. Two columns reached the Mitla Pass, winding some 14 miles through the mountains, so narrow the Israelis could move only three tanks abreast. But they had excellent aim, and even giving dug-in Egyptian tanks first shot, smashed them from more than 3,000 yards away. The Eilat-Kuntilla light brigade had crossed 140 miles of desert in just 36 hours.

To the south Brigadier Sharon's troops, joined by more armor, pushed on toward Nakhl to block Egyptian troops fleeing from the wasteland between the Gulf of Aqaba and the Red Sea.

Cut off from the canal, the Egyptian troops abandoned their tanks. Infantrymen threw away their shoes and began walking homeward across the desert, the same sands the Holy Family had crossed fleeing into Egypt. Climbing over the dunes, the soldiers never knew whether an Israeli tank would be on the other side. Sometimes there was.

Sometimes there was just another dune . . . and another . . .

Some Egyptians still held out. At El Arish an Egyptian commando force attacked the encircling Israelis, machine guns flaming. They were killed. In the Gaza Strip, men of the ragtag Palestine Liberation Army were surrounded and shelled by 120-millimeter mortars.

"Egypt will fight on," a Cairo spokesman said.

But in Israel, Major General Rabin said, "The Egyptians are defeated. All their efforts are aimed at withdrawing behind Suez

Forcing St. Stephen's Gate into the Old City

and we are taking care of that. The whole area is in our hands. The main effort of the Egyptians is to save themselves."

Said Dayan: "As far as the war between Nasser and our forces, the tragedy—the tragicomedy—is that in order to prove he is a paper tiger, you have to go to war."

At 10 A.M. that day, the Israelis dealt finally with the Gulf of Aqaba and the blockade that started the war. Israeli torpedo boats landed at Sharm el Sheikh, the Egyptian outpost at the head of the Straits of Tiran. The post was deserted. Paratroopers scheduled to jump landed at the airstrip

instead. The Egyptians had fled into the desert.

In Cairo, the radio declared, "We are not afraid of President Johnson. The Egyptian nation and guerillas will fight you and Israel." But there were others in the city whose fighting was over. Trucks that had proudly made their way through the city less than a month ago were returning, crowded with dusty, unshaven soldiers, still in battle dress. Youngsters climbed aboard and kissed the soldiers and slapped them on the back. But along the Nile, troops were digging trenches.

Back in Jerusalem in a ward of the Hadassah Medical Center, a Yemenite Jew, member of a tribe that had known great suffering in making its way to the Promised Land where it filled mostly menial jobs, lay wounded on a bed. He woke from a sleep, brought by drug and tormented with nightmare, and reached toward his left leg. The nightmare was true. It was gone.

"Nurse! Nurse!" he called. There was a clattering of heels in the corridor until a Yemeni-speaking nurse could be found.

"Nurse," he said, "tell them if we must fight for the Old City again, I still have another leg."

■ For the 1,349th time in its existence, the United Nations Security Council was called into session. The Soviet representative, Ambassador Fedorenko, had an urgent resolution to offer.

The problem was that the cease-fire resolution of the previous day was not being heeded. Israel's Ambassador Raphael said his country welcomed the resolution but its implementation depended on its acceptance by the other side. The only nation on the other side to accept was Jordan. Jordan had had enough. The Jordanian minister of foreign affairs, Ahmed Toucan, had been in telephone contact with New York when the resolution was passed and dispatched orders immediately to stop shooting unless shot at. Israel, complained Jordanian ambassador Muhammad H. el Farra, continued shooting and this very morning had seized the headquarters of the UN's Jordanian-Israeli Mixed Armistice Commission. Ambassador el Farra called it a calculated Israeli plot to grab more territory. For the past hour, however, all was reported quiet on the eastern front, but nowhere else. Soviet Ambassador Fedorenko decided it was time to set a deadline.

"On its part," he told the Council members, "the Soviet Union deems it essential that the Security Council, without any delay, demand as a first step a cease-fire of all military activities on June 7 at 2000 hours Greenwich Mean Time. The delegates glanced at their watches. That was less than an hour off—4 P.M. in New York, 10 P.M. in Jordan, 11 P.M. in Egypt and Syria.

The Council adopted the resolution unanimously and cables went out to the warring countries.

Israeli Foreign Minister Abba Eban said his country would agree, but, again, would stop shooting only if its enemies did the same. The deadline passed. As evening wore on reports began coming back from the Middle East. Egypt rejected the resolution. So did Syria. So did Iraq, Saudi Arabia, Algeria and Kuwait, where there was no fighting going on, anyhow. Only Jordan reaffirmed its acceptance.

Meanwhile, in shuttered and padlocked embassies through the Middle East, American diplomats burned secret papers while angry threatening mobs crowded the streets outside and jeered. The list of nations that had joined Egypt in breaking diplomatic relations with the United States had grown to six—Algeria, the Sudan, Syria, Iraq, Yemen and Mauritania. Lebanon had decided not to break relations but to show its displeasure with the United States by an abrupt recall of its ambassador.

The diplomatic ruptures were mainly in response to Nasser's claim that America and Britain had intervened in the war. The Soviet Union, for its part, continued to disregard the charge. In fact, for 24 hours Russia's tightly controlled press and radio did not even mention it. When it finally did, it mentioned only a claim of British intervention, not American, and published Britain's denial.

Arab countries also retaliated against the West with their economic weapon, oil. Libya, Saudi Arabia, Kuwait, Iraq and Algeria announced they were stopping oil shipments to the United States and Britain.

To cope with the growing Mid-East headaches and help put an end to the fighting, President Johnson formed a special committee of the National Security Council. To head it he recalled McGeorge Bundy, a former White House assistant, and called

Clad in armor, the Jews returned to their Wall.

WELCOME TO BETHLEHEM.

Central Front Commander Usi Narkiss and Defense Minister Moshe Dayan.

on all government agencies to supply the committee with staff support.

The efforts in Washington were impressive. So were those at the United Nations. But the war went on.

As Nasser's charge of American intervention spread through Egypt, mobs became a menace in every large city. The American Library in Port Said was sacked, and angry rioters attacked U.S. consulates in Port Said and Alexandria. The consular staff in Alexandria huddled in a security vault for more than four hours while a mob raced through the building burning curtains and furniture.

The American Embassy staff in Cairo faced other problems.

When Undersecretary Foreign Minister El Fekky notified U.S. Ambassador-designate Nolte that Egypt had severed diplomatic relations, he told Nolte that 96 American Embassy personnel could stay behind. These would be consular officers for the most part. This was standard diplomatic procedure.

But El Fekky later cut the figure down to five people. At that, the U.S. Deputy Chief of Mission in Cairo, David Nes, countered with a proposal that 24 officers and 37 support personnel remain. When Nes returned Wednesday evening to see whether the

Foreign Ministry accepted his offer, he was told the requirement had changed again: only four Americans could stay. All the rest, Nes was told, were blackballed as "security risks and probably CIA-oriented." As it turned out, Egypt finally agreed to let five remain— one American officer, two code clerks and two administrative employees—to be selected by Nasser himself.

■ In Pardess Hana, Ahmad Ben Essa did not report for work again for the second day at the home of Matan and Simcha Goor. A messenger came from the local military headquarters and told Simcha that her husband had been wounded. She left the children with her mother and set out for Jerusalem.

In the cool, breeze-swept wards of the Hadassah Medical Center, where helicopters were still landing on the lawn near the maternity clinic, word spread quickly that the Old City had been taken. Even the Arab Legionnaires, lying on their pallets in the corridor alongside fallen Israeli paratroopers, knew that the six-pointed blue Star of David was flying from the dun-gray walls.

110

Transistor radios spread the word from ward to ward, floor to floor. General Shlomo Goren, Torah in hand, was at the Wailing Wall, in his official capacity as Chief Rabbi of the Israeli armed forces.

"On our blood we took an oath," he was saying, "That we will never give it up, we will never leave this place. The Wailing Wall belongs to us. The holy place was our place first, our place and God's place. From here we do not move. Never. Never."

Men without arms and without legs were sitting up in bed weeping. Men were weeping from eyes that would never see again, and the nurses were weeping with them, for them.

The doors of one of the nine surgical theaters swung open, and Captain Matan Goor, part-time paratrooper, full-time biology teacher, was wheeled out. After a two-hour operation, the doctors had saved his leg. Barely conscious and under heavy sedation, he reached down and knew it was still there.

A pretty nurses' aide in a crisp blue miniskirt went by, rolling a cartload of books and magazines. The most popular item was Moshe Dayan's *Diary of the Sinai Campaign*.

The transistor radios blared out a march, the one from *The Bridge Over the River Kwai*. Captain Goor closed his eyes and slept for 10 hours. It was the first real rest he had had in four days. When he awoke, Simcha was standing at his bedside.

"Don't tell the children," he said, pointing to the heavily bandaged leg.

Then, before drowsing off again, he had another request: "Try to find Chico. I have to thank him."

■ Jerusalem was falling, and now the movement of refugees was in the opposite direction, away from the advancing army. Arab metalsmiths and tea merchants and souvenir sellers were shuttering their shops in the winding, narrow bazaars of the Old City, loading up their donkeys and camels and streaming out of the Moslem quarter, through the Damascus Gate and Herod's

Jerusalem embraces General Rabin, Israel's Chief of Staff.

Gate. They were leaving their tiny apartments and incredibly cramped little houses in the sloping arched streets and alleyways. They were fleeing the bombs that already were falling in the surrounding hills, the fire-belching tanks moving ponderously, unrelentingly, over the highways to the north and south in a murderous pincer that would encircle the Old City in a few hours.

Their movement was east; east on the main road to Amman, east through the Judean hills, east across the Jordan, east away from the thunder and the devastation, the night fires in the hills, the horror and the death, away from the Jews, away from the hated enemy. They took with them all that their wives and donkeys could carry, leaving behind food still warm on the table, pictures on the wall of bearded and robed ancestors, trunks full of the treasures and trivia of several lifetimes on those decaying cobblestoned streets.

Before the telephone lines went down, Rashid Areikat got a call in his office at the UNWRA refugee camp on the outskirts of the oasis city of Jericho. It was from his aging mother in Jerusalem. She was setting out on the road, by foot, to join him, a two-day journey under the broiling June sun. Rashid begged her not to come, but the old woman was consumed by fear and hysteria and loneliness. The planes were streaking in and out among the terraced hills, and artillery was rumbling in the nearby streets, rattling her windows.

Unable to stop her, Rashid Areikat set out to meet his mother on the road from Jerusalem. He climbed into his UNWRA car and sped down the road, weaving in and out among the clanking tanks and half-tracks rumbling to the rescue of the Old City. Rashid had driven only several miles out of town, when a flight of Mystères came streaking in over the flat floor of the desert from the vicinity of the Dead Sea. Suddenly he found himself hemmed in between two Iraqi tanks as the jets began their strafing run along the road. He jumped out of his car and rolled into a ditch.

With his face pushed into the dirt, Rashid could hear the belly-guns, hemstitching the road; he could hear the tearing sound of the rockets ripping apart the tank bodies and feel the heat of the burning vehicles. He thought of his mother, 30 miles away, on the road down from Jerusalem. When he finally climbed out of the ditch, after several minutes that seemed like hours, he saw his automobile smashed between the two smoldering tanks, caught in a ricochet of giant bits of shrapnel. The tank crews were sprawled in the roadway, all dead. They had climbed out too late.

Rashid walked back to camp and found frightening chaos. The refugees were screaming for food to take with them on the flight across the Jordan, and when his clerks refused, they threatened to burn down the camp. They were already trying to ignite a warehouse. Rashid sighed and gave them

An Israeli consoles the wound and tears of defeat.

112

what they wanted. He could easily feel for them. Homeless in the camp for 19 years, they were homeless again, heading east across the Jordan to what? New camps for the homeless?

■ For Kibbutz Ein Gev, Wednesday was the day its luck changed. The heavy shelling from the Syrian heights began a little after nine in the morning and continued almost without letup through the day. One burst of artillery rounds fell among the cattle sheds, killing eight prize calves. Mortar shells damaged twelve apartments, including the doctor's house, which had been hit in the April 7 attack. The round hit in almost the same place, up near the roof gables. Then an artillery round burst near the canning factory, killing one soldier and

wounding seven. None of the casualties were members of the kibbutz. All were part of a reserve infantry unit that had moved in a day before to help defend the border areas.

The kibbutzniks in the trenches ran out to help bring in the wounded. Among the first to volunteer for the hazardous assignment were Jean Claude Carrasset, from France, and Reinhold Forntail, from Germany. Both were gentiles, students at the Ulpan Hebrew school which the kibbutz operated.

Forntail helped bring in one of the wounded soldiers, dragging him down to the shelter, then headed out again, just as another barrage came crashing in.

"Don't go, now," cried Gershon Fine, his Hebrew teacher. "You'll be killed."

Forntail shrugged. "If I would be killed," he said, "it would be the smallest I could

In Bethlehem, Israeli armor pauses at the spot where the Prince of Peace was born.

do to atone for all that the Nazis did." He disappeared out the door.

As the bombardment of the border kibbutzim increased, Radio Syria stepped up its invective.

In the crowded shelter of Ein Gev, they gathered around the transistor radio to hear a Syrian announcer say in Hebrew:

"You are miserable Jewish people. We will pluck out the other eye of your Moshe Dayan. He will be blind, and it will be the blind leading the blind. Your army is surrendering everywhere. Jerusalem is burning. Tel Aviv is wiped out. Kill the bastard Zionists."

Gershon Fine shook his head. "Atrocious Hebrew," he said.

Fortunately, there were other diversions down in the shelter, where nerves were wearing a bit thin after nearly three days of communal incarceration. No longer could the wardens keep the people from running over to the doorway to look out every time the planes went over. They had been down there long enough to know the planes were friendly, because flight after flight screamed in from the west across the lake. Never once did they hear a Syrian plane go over, so they knew Kol Yisrael was accurate in reporting that the Arab air forces had been wiped out. From the steps of the shelter, they could see the Golan hills, a riot of spring flowers just a few weeks ago, all pink and blue and lavender, but now almost entirely blackened by constant baths of napalm.

Still the guns barked and the mortar tubes belched devastation from the fortified positions in the hills.

During the worst of it, when the shelter quivered as if in an earthquake and the air was a constant percussive symphony of exploding shells, Gershon Fine tried to keep the seven- to ten-year-old children in his care occupied with stories. He read them the fairy tale of the Happy Prince, and then some tales from Hans Christian Andersen. With his heavy asthmatic breathing, he read from a variety of books.

Once, when the rounds were falling in thumping clusters and the jets were whining low over the empty buildings, he read them a favorite passage he had saved for just such a moment:

"In spite of everything, I still believe that people are really good at heart. If I look up into the heavens, I think that it will all come right, that this cruelty, too, will end, and that peace and tranquility will return again."

The lines were written, several wars ago, by a 14-year-old girl named Anne Frank, who hid in an Amsterdam attic two years before she was carried off to the gas ovens of Auschwitz.

That night Kibbutz Ein Gev took the wounded out across the Sea of Galilee. The medics used the same boat that only a few weeks ago had brought throngs of happy tourists across those same placid waters to see Margot Fonteyn and the Royal Ballet perform in the annual Passover program. But now there were no running lights on the boat, and the motor had been geared down to its lowest, quietest speed to keep the Syrian artillerymen from zeroing in on a new target.

■Colonel Mohamed Galal wasn't fully aware of how bad his situation was on the third day of the battle in the Sinai. Nor, indeed, was he at all sure what the Egyptian army expected of his artillery brigade.

He had had no word from higher headquarters since 8 o'clock last night when he was told to hold his position at Wadi el Arish. That order came two and a half hours after he had been commanded to pull out of the wadi, move the brigade back to beleaguered Bir Hasana and then north to Libni. Colonel Galal couldn't understand why the order to move had been countermanded. He talked it over with his officers and all tended to agree it might mean a frontal attack from El Quseima was imminent.

The brigade had taken a beating. All day Tuesday Israeli planes, unopposed in the sky, straffed and bombed Colonel Galal's position and he had no antiaircraft guns to

Egyptian prisoners under Israeli guns

drive them off. His men shot back with rifles and machine guns but only felt puny and defenseless.

Again and again they asked the same question Egyptians all over the desert were asking: "Where are our planes?"

Colonel Galal's three dozen 122-millimeter howitzers were untouched by the air attacks. Their muzzles still pointed east, toward the Israeli border. And they were still unfired. The Israeli planes appeared to be going after trucks, not guns, and especially gasoline trucks. Casualties were not severe. Colonel Galal had lost six men, and four were wounded. One of the wounded lost both hands.

The brigade had been without supplies since the war began and food and water were desperately low. Colonel Galal sent a captain back to Bir Hasana to fetch water. The captain did not return. Later an ambulance with wounded men also struck out for Bir Hasana. It didn't return.

Tuesday, the sky over Bir Hasana, five miles to the rear, glowed through the night.

And along the road to the north Colonel Galal saw a steady stream of headlights creeping back from the front. The Egyptian army was pulling back. Colonel Galal could only surmise that his job was to cover the withdrawal.

Now it was 6 A.M. Wednesday and Colonel Galal was becoming desperate.

A messenger brought word that the anti-aircraft battery to the rear of his unit was out of ammunition. Where were the supplies?

Just after sunup, a jeep approached from the front, zigzagging up the valley. Galal knew the driver, an old military academy classmate, who reported that the front line forces were in full retreat. Galal gave his friend some water and suggested he go to Bir Hasana, cautioning him to stay off the road. Minutes later the officer was back. He said he had spotted Israeli tanks at Bir Hasana.

The Israelis had somehow got behind Galal's position and Bir Hasana was in enemy hands. It meant there would be no supplies. It also meant Colonel Mohamed

Surrender at El Arish

Galal's artillery brigade was cut off, its retreat blocked, trapped in the desert with little hope of relief and the water almost gone. Colonel Galal decided not to tell his men of their plight.

At 10 A.M. a forward observer spotted Israeli tanks, about 20 of them, approaching from the east.

"Are you sure they're Israeli tanks and not our own?" Colonel Galal asked. The observer said he was sure.

The Colonel considered his possibilities. Should he lay down an artillery barrage? If he did, reckoned Galal, surely the tanks would simply back out of range and call in the airplanes. Should he wait for the tanks to get close and engage them in a point-blank fire fight? You can't fight rapid-firing tanks with slow-loading artillery pieces, he reasoned.

He decided there was only one thing to do. Get out.

He gave the orders. His men loaded a shell in the breech of each howitzer, jammed a second shell down each muzzle, and fired the guns from trenches with ropes tied to the triggers. The colonel cringed as each gun exploded. Then they gathered all their communications equipment in a pile and riddled it with machine-gun bullets.

Galal loaded his men into 20 lorries and three jeeps. He took the lead jeep, drove it himself, with a major at his side and a half-dozen men in the rear.

The convoy had enough food for two days but only enough water for a few hours. It was 2 P.M. and the desert heat was intense. Colonel Galal led the column south across the sand for 25 miles, then west. His aim was to keep well south of the road while traveling as far west as he could, thus ducking any Israeli troops coming in from the north. When he thought he had gone far enough to the rear he would get back on the road again and head for the Mitla Pass. Surely the Israelis could not have penetrated that far yet.

Probing the desert in his jeep a half-mile ahead of the column, with a second jeep following behind, Colonel Galal picked up the road at a point he thought to be

A pause for prayer at the Wailing Wall

about 35 miles from Mitla. The jeeps bounced onto the gravel road and started up a rise.

At the crest, Galal suddenly whipped the wheel and spun the jeep to the right. Dead ahead, two Israeli tanks and a half-track stood poised in the road. The jeep lurched off the shoulder of the road just as the machine guns opened up. Galal dove out the door into the sand. He looked back. Both jeeps were like sieves and men lay bleeding on the road and in the jeeps. Galal saw a bullethole in his pants leg. He felt down; the leg was uninjured.

The firing continued. Colonel Galal whipped out a handkerchief, a green one, and waved it in surrender. The firing did not stop. He got to his feet, hands upraised, and went toward the tanks. The firing stopped. Galal heard an Israeli call out in Arabic, "Come, come, come."

Colonel Mohamed Galal went, and the Israelis took him prisoner. On the trip back across the Sinai, toward Israel and incarceration, Colonel Galal saw three lorries in flames by the side of the road. He did not know what had happened to his men. He wondered if the lorries were theirs.

Thirsting in Sinai, Egyptians surrender.

THURSDAY

"REQUEST PERMISSION TO WASH FEET . . ."

■ The pace of the Israeli army was stunning. In three days, it had smashed King Hussein's Arab Legion, erased the Jordanian bulge, and captured the sacred city, Jerusalem. And now, on Thursday, it blocked the retreat of the Egyptian army in the Sinai, and slammed shut the lid on the desert coffin.

Time and again, Egyptian tanks regrouped in the desert and dashed at the three passes that stood between them and escape. Time and again, Israeli guns blazed away from positions in the passes and with aircraft left the Egyptian armor black and smoking along the roads. In desperation, Egyptian jet fighters came out in the open, and tanks were barged across the Suez to try to clear the passes from the other end. It was futile. The Israeli air force swept the Egyptian planes from the air, and joined Israeli gunners from El Qantara to Mitla Pass in picking off the tanks like flightless, waddling ducks along the Suez Canal. There were five major battles Thursday, reportedly involving some 1,000 tanks, at these gateways to Suez. All ended in complete defeat for the Egyptians.

Then, suddenly, it was over. No fantasy, no wishful make-believe, no propaganda could change it. Gamal Abdel Nasser, after four days of feeding his people nothing but good news when the facts were nothing but bad, now had to admit, finally, that his Sinai adventure had failed. He gave up shortly before midnight, Thursday, June 8. Egypt accepted the UN cease-fire.

During the day, Israeli army headquarters

received an urgent message from the commander of an Israeli column in the far west.

"Request permission to wash feet . . ."

The headquarters commander began to boil. Some kind of joke? Some stupid new code?

He read on. He smiled.

"In the Suez Canal."

Permission was quickly granted.

And that was how Israel learned its troops had reached the Canal. And ironically, the war that began with Egyptian guns blockading traffic on the Gulf of Aqaba, seeking to choke off Israel from the Red Sea, that war now ended with Israeli guns trained on an even more crucial channel, the Suez Canal.

Here in four days of fighting, the biggest, strongest segment of the noose Nasser had been tightening around Israel for 19 years, now lay shredded, charred and useless. For all practical purposes, Nasser's vaunted army now lay dead in an area 100 miles wide and 150 miles long. Some 20,000 Egyptians had perished.

The final chapter began early Thursday. Israeli tanks already stood at the verdant old city of El Qantara that straddles the Suez Canal. In rapid order, another Israeli column reached the canal shore at Ismailiya and at Little Bitter Lake, and other forces faced the city of Suez. Then they fanned out along the canal. From the city, a column plunged south, along the Gulf of Suez toward the Red Sea. At Abu Zenima, about midway down the peninsula, it linked up with a unit which had started at Sharm el Sheikh at the tip of the peninsula. Now, for all practical purposes, the Sinai was in Israeli hands.

Only mopping up remained. Some Egyptians gave up easily.

One Israeli tank commander brought his unit over a dune to discover eight Egyptian tanks. Israeli gunners hit one immediately. The rest retreated. Then another was hit. Suddenly, the crews of the remaining tanks raised their hatches and fled on foot.

Outside of El Qantara, where one of the biggest tank battles took place, tank commander Amos Unger, 21, said he had heard a Russian-speaking voice on his radio giving

tactical instructions to Egyptian tankers. It was not the first such report. Captain David Petel, a paratrooper who speaks Russian, said he had intercepted messages from Russian advisors to Egyptian tanks at Khan Yunis in the Gaza Strip.

Only nightfall brought the Egyptian stragglers on the desert respite from the fury of Israeli jet fighter-bombers. And only nightfall covered the carnage. In the wake of the Israeli advance lay long lines of burned-

out and bombed Egyptian tanks, trucks, half-tracks, command cars and jeeps. The desert itself gave off the ugly smell of death, fetched by the dry, sandy wind. Flies swarmed over the dead and the living alike. They flew so thick, soldiers had trouble keeping them from their eyes and their mouths. The temperature ranged up to more than 120 degrees, and the north wind picked up the sand from the crest of dunes and drove it in the faces of men. Israeli soldiers salvaged

Egyptian gas masks, cut away everything but the eye-pieces, to make weird but effective goggles against it.

A Bedouin camel caravan stretched along a dune line, like an expensive Christmas card. But on closer look, the Bedouin drivers lay dead in the sand, and the camels and caravan dogs stood vigil over them. All along the roads were the signs of violence, blackened bodies and napalmed trucks. The Israelis sent for bulldozers to bury the dead before the bodies could breed epidemics to plague the living.

And now the long Israeli supply columns began to catch up with the spearheads. They found Egyptians bound and sitting in the shade of water towers along the coastal railroad, and they found others with hands in the air being marched into hastily enclosed barbed-wire structures. And they saw some blindfolded so they couldn't observe the Israeli movements and gauge their strength. They saw abandoned vehicles and discarded Egyptian boots, testifying to how many had run off into the desert.

And for the Egyptian straggler, the desert was an open tomb. One knelt by the road, begging passing Israeli trucks for water. His tongue was turning black, and his lips thick

as baked clay. He babbled incoherently, and fell foward on the sand. On the distant dunes, the Israelis saw small groups of Egyptians scrambling over the sand. No one bothered to chase them. "They will be caught sooner or later," said an Israeli officer. "Or else they will lay down their arms and try to swim to the west bank of the canal. In which case we will not bother them."

All along the desert, the approaches to small towns were marked with slit trenches and concrete pillboxes in the dunes. And these were blackened often with napalm. The towns were largely empty, and starving mongrels traveled in packs looking for food.

Near Suez, the Israelis found an Egyptian missile base intact in the desert. It was complete with unused missiles, radar and

The vanquished

122

cannon-pocked van. The missiles and equipment were Russian-made and used as ground-to-air defense. At least one had been fired at Israeli jets. But the missiles were meant for high altitude targets, and the Israeli planes came in at ground level.

At the other end of the desert, where the fighting began, in the dusty Gaza Strip, the final shreds of the Palestine Liberation Army were cleared away. And finally, the refugee-soldiers returned to the homeland they sought, to Israel that once was Palestine, where they were set to work building prisoner of war stockades for themselves and for others who were to follow.

In the far north, the seething border with Syria had drummed since Monday with volleys of bombs and shells. Now it was building to crescendo. The frustrations and hatreds of that already bloody frontier were about to explode into invasion.

But in Amman, for King Hussein, there was only defeat. Looking haggard, he announced his nation's losses: 15,000 dead.

"But we are proud of the fact we fought honorably," he said. "We are proud of our men and of the fact that despite all odds, we were able to stand like men, not only in the front line but also at home . . . I hope people all over the world will recognize the efforts this country made to defend its soil."

Even on the last day of the Sinai campaign, it was dangerous to get too close.

A gray, single-stacked ship, once a cargo ship and now heavy with electronics gear but light with visible menace, steamed westward some 15½ miles off the Sinai coast in the Mediterranean. Her name: The *U.S.S. Liberty,* a technical research ship. Her ostensible purpose: to aid, with communications, Americans trapped in embattled nations and trying to get out. But the ship was so equipped it could have eavesdropped on radio transmissions from both Israel and Egypt. The Defense Department denied that this was her mission.

But the *Liberty's* presence where she was, and a misdirected message that would have ordered her farther out to sea, set up the tragic circumstances of Thursday afternoon.

On the morning of June 8, the ship was cruising through international waters in a "condition of readiness three." That meant that her two 50-caliber machine guns aft were manned, and bridge crews stood by to man her two 50s forward in the event of a surprise attack. Those four guns were all she had.

At about 10:30 A.M., two unidentified jet aircraft circled the ship three times at an altitude of some 10,000 feet. To the south, the *Liberty's* crew could see a propeller-driven craft patrolling over the low Sinai coast.

Less than half an hour later, a cargo plane crossed astern of the *Liberty* about five miles away and then circled back for a closer look before heading for the Sinai Peninsula. Every 30 minutes the same plane came back to watch the *Liberty's* movements.

At 2 P.M., two jets arrived on the scene at about 7,000 feet. One flew parallel to the ship's seaward side. Then, suddenly, there was a loud explosion on the landward side of the *Liberty.* Rocket fire from a jet set afire two 55-gallon drums of gasoline used for fire-pump engines.

A bomb hit on the starboard side behind the bridge, and knocked officers and men in the pilothouse off their feet. Immediately, Commander William L. McGonagle of Norfolk, Virginia, sounded the general alarm, called for full speed, and ordered a message be sent to the Chief of Naval Operations, reporting the ship under attack and needing help.

The attacks continued, the planes criss-crossing the ship with strafing fire at 45- to 60-second intervals. Internal communications were knocked out. Runners took messages back and forth. Fire-fighting details and repair parties set to work. Behind the bridge, a whaleboat was blazing from the bomb hit. The attack lasted just barely over five minutes.

Commander McGonagle was hit by flying shrapnel and stunned. He noted slight burns "on my starboard forearm," and blood oozing from his right leg. But he could walk, and he carried on.

Just as the air attack was ending, three torpedo boats came in sight in what appeared

Wounded U.S. sailor from the Liberty.

to be attack position. They were approaching from the northeast at high speed. Commander McGonagle ordered his forward machine gunner, the only one who could hear him shout, to "take the boats under fire."

It was then he noticed that the ship's flag had been shot away. He ordered a holiday-sized ensign hoisted, measuring seven by 13 feet. He tried to alert the crew for torpedo attack, but with communications out, it was difficult. He knew there were shoals on his left. He could not turn toward land. And if he tried to turn the other way, he would only present the torpedo boats with a larger target.

Commander McGonagle now saw that the center boat was apparently trying to signal. It was flying an Israeli flag. But because of the smoke and fire on the *Liberty,* he couldn't read the signals. He tried to shout to the forward machine gunner to hold his fire. But by the time the gunner understood, he had already fired a short burst at the boats.

When the aft gunner heard the forward guns open up, he fired, too, and the fire was "extremely effective," blanketing the area and the center boat. An officer hurried aft to tell the gunner to cease fire, but there was no one there. Flames had already forced the crewman to leave his post. Now the Israeli boats opened fire, and a torpedo flashed away astern of the *Liberty.* One minute later, another torpedo, this one unseen, smacked into the starboard side forward, tearing a 39-foot hole in the converted World War II Liberty Ship. Twenty-five men were killed outright by the blast, and water was pouring in fast. The hatch had to be closed, sealing off the compartment and its men.

The torpedo boats now stopped still in the water. They milled around some 800 yards astern of the *Liberty.* One flashed a signal light asking in English, "Do you require assistance?"

By now the *Liberty* had no way to answer. She hoisted code flags Lima India to show she was having difficulty maneuvering and other boats should stay clear.

About 3:15 P.M., two helicopters arrived at the scene and circled the ship some 100 yards off. Insignia showed they were Israeli. At about the time they arrived, the torpedo boats left. The helicopters moved some five miles away and then darted back again at high speed. At the same time two more jet planes appeared, and the ship had another attack scare.

Commander McGonagle, weak from loss of blood, lay on his back in the bridge. From here he messaged the Sixth Fleet. The answer said help was on the way at flank speed.

At 6:41 P.M., an Israeli helicopter arrived and hovered 30 feet above the bridge. It signalled visually that it wanted to land a man aboard. Because the ship was so cluttered with debris, McGonagle had the copter waved away. It returned a few minutes later and dropped a parcel on deck. It was a calling card from Commander Ernest Carl Castle, naval attaché for air at the U.S. Embassy in Tel Aviv. On the back was a message: "Have you casualties?"

The ship tried to answer with light signals, but after 15 minutes of unsuccessful attempts, the helicopter left. McGonagle, now on the verge of unconsciousness from loss of blood, got emergency medical help. Then he steered his ship through the night by watching its wake. Later it joined up with Sixth Fleet destroyers.

A naval court of inquiry found that the U.S. vessel was properly marked as to identity and nationality. It could find no reason for the attack. The Israeli government, which apologized immediately, sought the answers, too. It gave the facts of its investigation to an officer of the court empowered to convene courts-martial. But the questions that persisted were: what was the *Liberty* really doing? Was it a tragic mistake and only that? The stricken ship limped away from the battle scene with 34 dead and 75 wounded.

■ President Johnson was still in his bedroom, though he had been at work for three and a half hours, when the first startling news of the attack on the *Liberty* came shortly after 10 A.M. It was not known who had done the attacking, but planes from the Sixth Fleet were streaking to the scene.

The President phoned the Situation Room. He instructed his staff to draft a note to Soviet Premier Kosygin, to be sent on the hot line, advising the Premier of the attack and assuring him the American planes were not on a hostile mission.

As the note was being transmitted, Israel sent the U.S. official notice that it was responsible for the attack and had acted in error. President Johnson sent Premier Kosygin a second note relaying this information.

During the afternoon word began to leak out that the hot line had been put to use during the past few days. To forestall mis-

chievous rumor, the President decided to acknowledge the fact, and so messaged Kosygin. That out of the way, the President turned his attention to the United Nations.

There, both U.S. Ambassador Goldberg and Soviet Ambassador Fedorenko were readying proposed resolutions for consideration by the Security Council. Goldberg's insisted that all parties heed the cease-fire and begin negotiations on troop withdrawals. Fedorenko's demanded that the Council condemn Israel as an aggressor and require its troops to pull back to its original borders. Mohamed Awad el Kony, the Egyptian ambassador, also was on the speaker's list. Before him on his desk was a 20-page draft.

Just after the meeting opened, El Kony

was summoned to the telephone. Cairo was calling. Back in the Council chamber, El Kony walked straight to the table and handed a message to Secretary-General U Thant. The faintest of smiles played briefly across the Secretary-General's impassive face as he scanned the message. In a dry, precise voice, he read the note aloud to the council members. The Egyptian government of President Gamal Abdel Nasser, said U Thant, had "decided to accept the cease-fire" called for in the United Nations resolutions." The time was 3:20 P.M. In Cairo it was 10:20 P.M., almost exactly 85 hours after the war began.

Jordan had quit. Egypt had quit. That left only Syria.

Ambassador Goldberg quickly revised his resolution. Looking to the future, he proposed that Israel and the Arab states enter into discussions for disengagement of all armed personnel and seek the help of the United Nations to get the critical talks underway as soon as possible.

At 9 P.M.—it was 4 A.M. Friday in Syria—the Syrian government sent a message to the Israeli-Syrian Mixed Armistice Commission in Damascus saying that Syria would observe the cease-fire. The Commission forwarded the message to Israel. But at that hour in New York the UN Security Council had already adjourned, though the Syrian representative did pass the word along to the Secretary-General.

Grim fighting lay ahead in the Syrian hills.

Israeli phosphorus shell blasts Syrian tank

FRIDAY

LOOK TO THE HILLS

■ For the Israelis now, it was two down, one to go. The fronts in Jordan and Egypt lay silent under a UN cease-fire. On Thursday, Syria, too, decided to get out before it faced Israel alone and accepted a cease-fire. But now, on Friday, the cease-fire fell apart and the border erupted once more. Before the day was out, Israeli infantry and tanks stormed the Syrian heights, the mountains of Golan, where Crusaders once held sway. When they stopped to rest that night, Israeli forces were poised in small pincers around Syrian fortifications that one officer called a little Maginot Line.

The campaign began on the northern end of the border. On the Israeli side, dug in and armed, were the kibbutzim, so often torn by Syrian guerilla raids and artillery shells. The Syrian positions in the mountains were a maze of camouflaged trenches and bunkers, lined with the black volcanic stone and cement, and covered with steel and dirt and wild grass. The trenches were eight feet deep and three feet wide and they led to large rooms carved out of the mountains during the last 19 years. According to the Israelis, the underground fortifications were dug by the Syrians on the advice of the Russians. At any rate, their mortars were Russian.

The assault began with concentrated artillery fire and aerial attack. Israeli jets pounded the mountains and seared them with napalm. An Israeli armored brigade fought its way up the heights and crossed the border at 11:30 A.M. In front of them,

an infantry patrol provided cover for engineers blasting a path for the tanks.

The fighting was fierce. The armored brigade split into two columns—one sweeping toward Zaura which it took by 4 P.M. The other pushed to Zovebb el Meiss, and then the two columns linked up again.

An Israeli infantry force of the Golani Brigade, backed by tanks, fought up the steep heights toward fortified positions at Tel Aziziyat, Tel Fahar, Burj-Babil and Bahariyat, and finally the village of Baniyas. But the fighting was hardest at Tel Fahar, a bluff two miles south of Baniyas and two miles east of the Israeli kibbutz at Dan. From their dug-in positions in the heights, the Syrians were firing into the hazy hills of Galilee and the fertile valley leading to them. The Israeli infantry attacked Tel Fahar at 6 P.M. Supporting tanks were slowed by the heavy fire from the trenches and bunkers, and by the mines sowed on the approaches. It became a job for the infantry, a dirty job of face-to-face fighting, and cutting through the coils of barbed wire. Finally Israeli troopers made it to the trenches and cornered the Syrians inside and the fighting was furious. It took three hours to dig them out. The Israeli troopers pushed through the catacombs to the command post, an underground room with kerosene lanterns, tables and chairs, maps on the walls, and sleeping rooms lined with double bunks and dull green footlockers. This one complex held 120 men. And there were hundreds of them along the Syrian ridges leading to snow-streaked Mount Hermon.

After the breakthrough, the Israeli troops began an encircling maneuver to the village of Qoufeira and beyond. Israeli tanks pushed on to Raouie.

South of these battles, Israeli infantry and paratroop units struck in a series of frontal assaults. They pierced the Syrian defense line at Jalibna, Dradra, Tel Hilel and Darbeshiya. Two prongs of this drive blasted out bridgeheads at Darbeshiya in the north and the customs house in the south. Then they stopped for the night, to reorganize, refuel and resupply.

Behind, in the border kibbutzim and in the towns, the area swarmed with Israeli troops and tanks all day Friday, flooding into the Syrian highlands. The people of the kibbutzim had been holed up in the shelters for protection from Syrian shellfire since Monday. Now they were hanging out blankets to air, and for the first time that week the *chavarim* ate in the dining hall at Dan. Captured Syrian weapons were stacked in piles, and officials of the kibbutz inspected the smashed windows and wrecked apartments. People talked excitedly of perhaps visiting captured Syrian villages, and there was a sense of relief knowing that the ominous mountains were now in Israeli hands.

Truckloads of soldiers moved east and north through the kibbutzim, and the convoys were the same ragtag assortment of vehicles that had moved off to supply the forces in Egypt. But instead of captured Egyptian trucks, these convoys pressed captured Jordanian vehicles into service. Some soldiers pulled off the road for breaks, and moved into the apple orchards to escape the suffocating heat. Girls of the kibbutzim waved to the men in the trucks and cheered and threw them oranges.

Transport was critical. Passing through towns, officers requisitioned vehicles to help resupply units. One was a van belonging to Olga Klein, a 57-year-old Russian immigrant who ran a little grocery store in Tiberias. Olga went along as the driver, making the perilous, winding drive along the shell-cratered road into Syria. The troops dubbed her "Mother Courage," because she regaled them with stories of the days when she drove an ambulance for the Red Army in the battle for Stalingrad.

The kibbutzim along this border were called the "trip wire" or first line of defense, and the Israelis there manned their own guns.

At Kibbutz Dan, Joseph Levari, 31, a high-school teacher, was manning the forward machine gun. Suddenly he saw Syrian soldiers, some of them wearing gas masks, advancing across the no-man's-land. The schoolteacher fired his machine gun and saw several Syrians fall. Then he heard tanks—new Soviet-built Syrian tanks—rolling down a ravine toward him. They were 400 yards off. He called in artillery fire. One tank was hit, a second broke down, and the third retreated. The Syrian infantry, without tank support, turned and ran.

■ In the desert there was no retreat, not from the hot sand and the unyielding sun, the mutual enemies of all the armies that ever marched across the land of Ishmael and Isaac. Corporal Kamal Mahrouss, put to rout by the Israelis at El Kuntilla, had been fighting his new enemy, the desert, for three days. It had not defeated him.

There were 16 others in the truck with Kamal when it bounced off the road into the night to escape the murderous Israeli tank fire. Next morning marauding Israeli jets spotted the truck rolling across the white sand and peeled off to attack. The men scattered. The planes destroyed the truck and took after the fleeing men. Two fell. Kamal and his friends wrapped both bodies in blankets, tagged them, and walked on.

Weak, aching with thirst, they stumbled onto an abandoned mine excavation—with a water well. They tried to sleep but heard dogs barking in the distance and feared they might belong to the enemy. With full canteens they pushed ahead, west by the compass, toward Suez.

Kamal Mahrouss husbanded his water

Some Egyptians, as Kamal Mahrouss, walked home.

but it was gone soon enough. His lips swelled and cracked, his throat burned. He gathered pebbles and sucked them. Desperate, he drank his own urine.

Somewhere in the Sinai wilderness a Bedouin, a nomad who over countless generations has come to terms with the desert, appeared and offered help. Kamal was about to pay him to lead them to Suez but then changed his mind. He decided his compass was more trustworthy and sent the Bedouin on his way. Weak to the point of exhaustion, the soldiers trudged on. By turns they fainted and had to help one another up and along.

From the top of a sand dune Kamal saw what appeared to be an army installation. The group, with new strength, started toward it. It was a rocket site. Inside, they found food and water. They drank and drank and then put their fingers in their throats and disgorged themselves and drank some more. Then they ate. Then slept.

It had been three merciless days. Now it was Friday and searchlights sweeping across the sky stirred Kamal Mahrouss from his sleep. He decided to leave. Stuffing his clothing with food and canteens of water, he struck out with three companions, two of them wounded. It was 4 A.M. Along the way they came upon six Egyptian soldiers, exhausted by the side of the road, begging for water. Kamal gave them water and fed them.

Suddenly the scream of jet engines chorused overhead and Kamal ran once more for cover but in the desert there is no cover. He just ran. The planes left. Kamal Mahrouss walked on.

■ Friday. The Moslem sabbath. The shops were closed in Cairo and the people idled in the streets and gathered beneath the loudspeakers to hear the latest news over Cairo Radio. They were restless, dispirited. The news had not been good.

At the Nile Hotel, the 250 interned Americans watched from their windows. They also noted that the motley platoon of soldiers

133

guarding the hotel had been replaced by tough security police carrying submachine guns. Why? Why?

Then the announcement came. Gamal Abdel Nasser would make a public statement, his first since the war started. The Americans clustered around transistor radios.

"Brothers," Nasser began, "we have become accustomed . . . to speak with open hearts and to tell each other the facts . . .

"We cannot hide from ourselves the fact that we have met with a grave setback in the last few days." Nasser continued, giving his version of the causes of the hostilities, repeating his charge of American and British intervention, commending the Jordanians and other allies, and finally getting to the main point:

"Does this mean we do not assume responsibility for the consequences of this setback? I tell you truthfully that I am ready to assume the entire responsibility. I have taken a decision with which I want you all to help me.

"I have decided to give up completely and finally every official post and every political role and to return to the ranks of the public to do my duty with them like every other citizen."

The streets exploded. In Tahrir Square, masses of Egyptians clad in long, flowing, peasant *galabyas,* waved their arms and chanted "Nasser! Nasser! Nasser!" Old women scooped up dust and threw it on their heads, as though in mourning. Soon, a million and a half Egyptians were surging through the streets, wailing and weeping. There were indications, however, that this mass outburst of emotion wasn't purely spontaneous: many of the demonstrators arrived at Tahrir Square in government busses and trucks.

Inside the Nile Hotel, the Americans could hear the roar of the mob echoing through the dark streets. Egyptian guards herded the internees into the basement. Outside, the shouting grew angrier, and fists pounded on two metal doors leading from the basement to the street. The Americans remained orderly though some women sobbed softly. From the streets, over the din

of the mob, came the sound of submachine gun fire and the thud of concussion grenades. The Egyptian security forces held the line outside the hotel, and in two and a half hours it was over. The mob moved on. Hours later the Americans heard the welcome news: they would be evacuated at 2 A.M.

Meanwhile, Nasser's "resignation" began taking shape as a ploy to win the popular support he needed to sustain him in defeat.

As his successor, Nasser had designated Vice-President Zakaria Mohieddin, an old army buddy from the 1948 Palestine war and a member of the revolutionary council that took control after the overthrow of King Farouk in 1952. Mohieddin got on the radio with an impassioned speech.

"Like other citizens of this nation," he said, "I accept no leadership but his leadership." He concluded: "As for myself, I do not accept the presidency."

For itself, the Egyptian National Assembly reacted likewise. It voted 360–0 not to accept the resignation. Later, by a similar vote, it gave Nasser full power "to mobilize all the popular forces and rebuild the country politically and militarily."

Nasser drafted a message to the Assembly:

"I wished, if the nation had helped me, to stand by my decision to resign. But no one can imagine my feelings at this moment in view of the people's determination to refuse my resignation. I feel that the people's will cannot be refused; therefore I have decided to stay where the people want me to stay until all traces of aggression are erased."

End resignation.

The streets of Cairo erupted in joy. The air rang with the *zagrouta,* the Arab woman's shrill cry of joy usually reserved for weddings and feasts.

And soon the Americans who had been interned in the Nile Hotel would be exulting, too. After an anxious trip to Alexandria, through jeering and spitting crowds, they boarded the *Carina II,* a Greek liner chartered by the American government to take them to Athens. And there before them, waiting as an escort just beyond Egypt's 12-mile territorial limit, lay a destroyer flying the Stars and Stripes. Their ordeal was over.

■ Across the ocean, the United Nations decided to try one more time.

The Security Council already had passed two cease-fire resolutions, but the war was still going on. The Egyptian and Jordanian fronts were silent, but on the Syrian front the fighting was furious—with both sides claiming they were simply acting in self-defense.

Now the Security Council had a third resolution. This one demanded an end to hostilities "forthwith." At 2:42 P.M. Syrian Ambassador George J. Tomeh announced that his government had agreed to lay down its arms, if Israel did. At 3:05 P.M. Israeli Ambassador Gideon Raphael said his country would stop fighting if Syria did.

At 4:25 the Council recessed, hoping to find out just which country was violating the cease-fire. At 7:21 P.M. it reconvened. Again, only this time in bitter, acrimonious language, each side accused the other. At length the Council adjourned. Perhaps by tomorrow, the Secretary-General said, there would be more reliable information from the battle area.

In Tel Aviv, Premier Levi Eshkol spoke with scarcely concealed irony. Discussing the fact that Israel had been asked to show restraint before responding to the Arab buildup around her in the days preceding hostilities, he recalled Eban's discussions then with American officials. The Premier said:

"They told us that 40 to 50 maritime powers would sign a guarantee for free passage through the Tiran Strait. . . . We examined the situation and found that it really came down to a dozen and finally to only two countries and then, perhaps, to only one—Israel . . .

"I once told President Johnson that it is likely that when we are attacked you will be very busy with other matters and that the nature of the guarantee is unclear."

■ All day long, under the merciless sun, the Arab refugee families moved east along the macadam road, war's river of sorrow, flowing

"Nasser! Nasser! Nasser!" they cried when their leader resigned.

toward the bombed out Allenby Bridge over the Jordan. At 6 A.M., when the curfew ended, they suddenly appeared, rising up from the robes in which they had wrapped themselves against the cold desert winds, like wraiths come to life from distant mirages over the sands.

Rashid Areikat, deputy area officer for UNRWA, stood in the doorway of his office watching them stream by the gates of Aqabat Jaber, one of the four refugee camps he administered. The war west of the Jordan was over, but for them the heartache had just begun. He saw whole Arab families, from feeble grandparents to tiny toddlers, moving in barefoot procession along the dusty road, erect, graceful people, toting all their belongings—bedding, gasoline stoves, pots and pans, enormous jars of water—on their heads. In that debilitating below-sea-level heat, with the Dead Sea shimmering in the distance like a burning blue coal in the yellow desert, some of the Bedouins had removed their *kefeyas* (desert headdresses) to hold the white cloth aloft as a flag of surrender.

Many of the pilgrims on that burning road wore two and three overcoats, several dresses or an extra pair of trousers, as the best method of transporting their entire wardrobe. Some of the women carried an infant in each arm, and were followed by a string of small children, each carrying a still smaller one. Docile donkeys, swaying camels and an occasional broken-down draft horse trotted along in the pathetic parade, laboring under great burdens of furniture, mattresses, wooden steamer trunks from voyages on ships long since scrapped.

They were heading east toward Amman and Al Karak, away from the lands now occupied by the Israeli army, into what was left of young King Hussein's kingdom. Rashid Areikat was powerless to stop them, just as he had been powerless to stop his own mother, who had arrived safely the night before, after walking two days from Jerusalem. Like her, many had come from homes they had lived in for years in the Old City and they had been on the road to Jericho for several days. They were fleeing from the war, from the fighting armies, but mostly from the Jews, an ancient enemy who had swept their armies aside in 47 hours of furious fighting.

Rashid Areikat had seen at least 50,000 of them pass his doorstep. Two days ago he had worried how he would set about feeding the 60,000 Palestinian refugees in his four camps. Now he had less than 15,000 left and enough food on hand to last six months. After years of yearning to go back to their ancient lands in old Palestine, they had suddenly left the camps to head even farther east across the Jordan.

The scene at the Allenby Bridge was as moving as any along the road. The Jordanians had blown up the bridge to keep the advancing Israeli army from crossing the river. The wrecked bridge's long concrete span dipped down from the high banks to the brackish green water in a perfect "V." To negotiate the precipitous span, which fell away before them like a garish ski slide, the fleeing Arabs had to hold onto hastily tied guy ropes, make their way across the stream on a few planks lashed together, then climb

A prayer for the future from the ruins of her home.

With all they could carry they left their homes.

up the other side of the span by pulling on the ropes.

For most, this meant selling their donkeys, camels and horses, which could not manage the perilous footing, and getting rid of much of the impedimenta that they had carried all the way from Jerusalem. At high noon, the west bank of the Jordan resembled an Arab bazaar, with the pilgrims arguing excitedly and angrily with buyers for a fair price for their animals. All around, there were donkeys and goats tied to every available tree, left behind by the fleeing Arab families, and the grassy shores were littered with piles of cast-off clothing, furniture, empty shoes, rusting gasoline cans. Every now and then, to underline the horror of it all, a body bobbed up in the greenish water, bloated and black. It belonged to one of the fleeing pilgrims who had stubbornly insisted on crossing the bridge as the Legionnaires were blowing it up.

Rashid Areikat watched them and won-dered what life awaited them on the opposite bank, probably another refugee camp, drab and grim, hastily constructed to satisfy a sudden emergency that would undoubtedly linger on and on, the old festering sore of the refugee problem spreading farther and farther east. He thought about his own nationality now.

He was born in Jerusalem, when the British administered it for the League of Nations. After the Jews carved out a new nation in 1948, he became an employee of the United Nations, a stateless citizen dedicated to housing the homeless.

Now the Jews were occupying the west bank of the Jordan River, and a New York-born paratrooper, Major Noam Launder, was residing in the governor's villa in Jericho with the title of Military Governor. They had gotten on well together, since Launder arrived two days ago, even if the major did keep referring to the west bank as "New Israel."

137

The major, a dapper little man, had shown compassion for the fleeing multitudes. On the same road where the Good Samaritan had cared for the dying traveller, the Israeli Military Governor sent army trucks to dole out water to the sun-scorched pilgrims. This morning, he commandeered Jericho's municipal buses to convey the women and children to the bridge.

Areikat knew, just as Major Launder knew, that every Arab crossing to the east bank was one less mouth to feed, one less problem to handle on the west bank. Most of the fleeing Arabs also knew that by order of the government of Israel, once they had crossed the Jordan there would be no crossing back. Soldiers were stationed all along the river bank to keep them from changing their minds.

The Allenby Bridge was the point of no return. Some reached the river bank after days of walking, and suddenly turned back, as if deciding there and then to take their chances with their Israeli conquerors. Some sat for hours under the gnarled, silver-gray olive trees, praying to Allah for guidance. But for most, the Jordan was their Rubicon and they crossed over willingly, determinedly, going back to Hussein's kingdom, leaving behind, perhaps forever, their dreams of one day returning to Old Palestine.

Late in the afternoon, with a molten sun burning into the Dead Sea's lunar landscape, the great sad solemn river of humanity dwindled to a trickle, and by 4 P.M., curfew time for the vanquished, the road to Jericho was empty.

Night came and the moon rose over the refugee camp, bathing the tin roofs in a ghostly glow. Three miles out of Jericho, where the river narrowed between sandy banks, four Israeli paratroopers crouched behind a 50-caliber machine gun pointed menacingly across the softly murmuring water. They were there to stop refugees from returning. A case of Gold Star beer, submerged in midstream but anchored to a tree, sparkled in the moonlight, just below a neatly painted sign that said in English:

"Traditional Site of the Baptism of Jesus."
And the Jordan rolled on.

Flight across the Allenby Bridge

139

SATURDAY

"HOW THE MIGHTY ARE FALLEN"

■ The bleak hills of Syria lay wrapped in the morning mists. The sky lightened perceptibly, but the first light was below the ridge and did not reach to the valleys of grain.

Then, with expected suddeness, the hills shook again with the sounds of war. Israeli jets tore through the sky and hurled napalm and high explosives at the Syrian positions, some of them dug 50 feet deep into the mountains. Now came the Israeli armor and infantry, on the move once more.

From the bridgeheads in Syrian territory, won so hard the day before, the Israelis cracked again into Syrian positions. A strong armored force hit at fortifications at Tel Hamra, and then cleared the area north to the Lebanese border, before turning east again toward Massada.

Southeast of the Sea of Galilee, paratroopers with tanks and half-tracks pushed up from Tel Katzir, up the Tewfik mountains. The Israelis helicoptered troops ahead to cut off the Syrian retreat, and leapfrogged up the road to Botamia. From Galilee itself, waves of infantry moved out from the entire shore.

In the center of the line, the Israeli troops jumped off at 10 A.M. from the narrow foothold around the Syrian underground fortresses. It was tough going Friday, and it was tough going today. Tank columns rolled up the heights to support the infantry. The Israeli air force kept up its bombardment.

Now all along the border, Israeli forces were pounding away ceaselessly at the Syrians in the hills.

The ancient Crusaders' castle at the heights near Kalat Namrud, already worn and toppled by time, was hit again by Israeli jets to smash Syrian mortar crews using it for cover.

At Tel Kafar, it took two hours of bombing and mortar barrages to pave the way for a frontal charge by a battalion of Israeli infantry. Even then Israeli losses were heavy, and the battalion commander was killed.

Some of the troopers had already weathered fighting in the Sinai, or in Jordan. Now they were thrown against a new enemy in new terrain. "The Syrians fight better than the Egyptians," said one veteran. But a young lieutenant, his submachine gun still smoking, disagreed. "They ran like rabbits when they saw our campaign hats," he said.

Syrian escape routes were littered with burned and blasted Syrian tanks, rifles, mortars, boots, even socks. Some of the Syrians, like the Egyptians in the Sinai, found it easier to flee barefooted.

In the distance, columns of smoke rose from the hills, and the sky was pocked with black blotches where Syrian ammunition and fuel dumps flared into the sky.

With devastating thoroughness, the Israelis scourged the area that had been a springboard for terrorists who had raided the kibbutzim since 1948. And with a vengeance they blew up the concrete and stone forts where Russian-made cannon and mortars were trained on the Israeli border.

One Israeli column drove south to Dera on the Jordanian-Syrian border to punish

140

Infantrymen scramble across Syria's rocky hills.

Palestinian raiders who had used the town as a training base for guerilla tactics.

Israeli soldiers rested where they could. In the areas where snipers still prowled, they took shelter behind sandbags and fallen trees. And they kept a careful eye on the surrounding hills. A glint of sunlight reflected off the pair of binoculars of a Syrian observor. A shot rang out. The glint disappeared.

Near the border, a young sergeant rested at the wheel of his jeep, his eyes bleary from how many sleepless nights.

"You know," he said, "this was to be my wedding night. Sarah and I were to be married, and here I sit. But I guess she'll wait for me."

She would not have long to wait.

After a morning of pounding, the Syrian line showed signs of collapse. Two Israeli columns, one from the north and one from the south, began to close, cutting off the retreat of Syrians within their embrace.

The pace of the Israeli drives picked up. Syrians abandoned encircled positions and fled toward the rear. The Israeli armor charged toward El Qunaytirah. They found the city all but deserted. Its 30,000 residents were gone. Only a handful of straggling Arabs remained. One, an old lady, was bound for a nearby village. Exhausted and frightened, she collapsed along the road. An Israeli jeep picked her up and took her to her destination.

Now columns of Israeli half-tracks, jeeps mounted with recoilless rifles, and tanks streamed over the macadam roads coiling up the Syrian hills. Behind them, filled with troops, came the same Tel Aviv buses that had carried men to other battles in the past five days.

Now they bounced over the tank-torn blacktop toward El Qunaytirah. Israelis were already in the modernistic Syrian Frontier headquarters building and officers drank toasts in captured champagne in the Syrian Officer's Club. Israeli vehicles of every description filled the otherwise deserted streets. Israeli troopers and tanks manned outposts five miles down the road, barely 30 miles from the Syrian capital. At

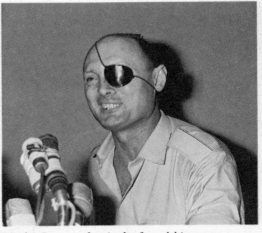

Moshe Dayan: the Arabs feared him most.

143

6:30 P.M., the Syrians agreed to the UN cease-fire.

Across the hills, there was the sporadic clatter of gunfire, less and less frequent now. Night came at last, and the war that exploded over Egypt and Israel Monday morning six days before—that consumed the lives of more than 35,000 men—flickered out Saturday night to a barely distinguishable ember.

■ The fighting had stopped for Major Jamil of the Arab Legion early Tuesday morning. But the war had not.

He lay in the Convent of the Sisters of Zion, a French order, which is next to the courtyard where Pontius Pilate washed his hands of the troublesome Galilean who had been brought before him. Jamil had been wounded in the leg by a machine gun bullet and now the wound was infected. He could not stand.

He was no longer wearing the proud uniform and red and white headdress of the Legion. On Wednesday, Arabs had told the sisters that the Israelis were shooting anyone found in uniform. Jamil and the wounded Legionnaires with him had burned their uniforms and put on clothing smuggled into the convent by civilian Arabs.

Jamil lay, in pain, on the pavement of the convent's basement. Nearby were flagstones that dated from the Romans and by tradition were the spot where the legionnaires of those days had cast dice for the robe of Christ.

The sisters had made bandages for the men and brought them food. The sisters were Christians as well as women. This was a man's war between Jew and Moslem, not theirs. And some men needed succor. They gave it.

Through the stone walls Jamil could hear Israeli sound trucks announcing that Nablus and Ramallah and other places west of the Jordan had fallen. Jamil didn't believe it.

Late Wednesday morning Israeli soldiers had come up to the convent firing Sten guns in the air, Jamil was told. That was when the sisters had moved him and the other wounded into the basement.

But early the next day the Israelis were back and entered the convent, carrying their weapons. The head of the convent, a French priest, faced the Jews and told them they should not be carrying weapons there. They turned and left.

The priest, who was also a doctor, took care of the Legionnaires as best as he could. Now, it was Saturday, and the priest was gone; he had left for Nazareth. The Israelis returned.

Jamil told his story:

"They tromped in like elephants, about 25 of them, three officers and a doctor. We were about eight or nine of us. They or- dered us out into the street to face the wall and searched us. I could not stand and crouched on the ground.

"Then they began shooting over our heads, to terrorize us, I suppose. They had driven a few Arab priests—novices actually—out with us and included them in the lineup. They shoved us into a truck and drove us outside the walls to a barbed-wire com-

A Syrian road is littered with death and destruction.

pound near the St. George Hotel. We thought they would take care of our wounds. Instead they tortured us with their harassment.

"We were lying on the ground. Hundreds of wounded and the dying had been brought from other hospitals. One man next to me had half his face shot away. Another had been thrown on the ground with his broken leg twisted under him. The sun burned down. The Israeli guards outside the wire laughed and shot over our heads. You could smell my wound 10 meters away. I planned to commit suicide by cutting my wrists with a razor blade if it came to a point where the Israelis recognized me as an officer. They would have killed me, anyway, in that case.

"After we had been in the compound for some hours, the soldiers came in and stole every valuable we had. Then they blindfolded us and took us to Jewish Jerusalem. They interrogated us. Two Jordanians made the mistake of saying they were soldiers.

They were taken away. We never saw them again."

The Israelis asked Jamil who he was. He said he was a farmer from Amman, which, in fact, he was as well as an officer, in Jerusalem on business.

"Who shot you?" they asked.

"You, of course. Who else?" he replied.

This seemed to satisfy the Israelis. They returned Jamil to the convent. The major wondered how he would reach the Jordan River, for the land between it and Jerusalem was no longer his. It belonged to the enemy. This he now believed.

■ Late Saturday afternoon, just as the sun was sinking as a golden ball into the Sea of Galilee, the heavy thrum of tanks and half-tracks brought the residents of Kibbutz Ein Gev streaming out of their trenches and shelters. They ran down to the gates of the kibbutz to watch the Israeli army make its farthest northern advance across the Jordan, past their burnt-out grain and bar-

Their faces told their story: defeat.

146

ley fields, up the napalm-blackened Golan heights into Syria. Standing at the bombed-out pillbox and the bullet-marked watchtower, where in the 1948 War for Independence they had fought for their land and lives, the kibbutzniks cheered and wept as the advancing army passed by. Its first objective, already heavily plastered by flight after flight of strafing jets, was Towfik, the heavily-fortified Syrian town from whose deeply emplaced concrete bunkers mortar and artillery shells had tormented the kibbutz for the past 19 years.

Although there was still heavy fighting ahead, the soldiers were in a jubilant, almost schoolboy mood. Fresh from the battle of Jerusalem and the sweep to the west bank of the Jordan, they flourished Jordanian wine flasks, brandished Arab daggers and bayonets and, on their tanks and half-tracks, displayed pictures of King Hussein upside down.

"On to Damascus," the kibbutz dwellers cried, and the children of Ein Gev ran into the road to give the troops water and candy.

The long line of tanks, some of them only yesterday the property of the Arab Legion, stretched as far as the eye could see up the winding road from the below-sea-level lake. It snaked around the base of Mount Tabor all the way to Megiddo along one of the classic battlegrounds of history. Here, in other ages and other wars on the great route from Cairo to Damascus, had come the elephants of Antiochus, the caravans of Cleopatra, the eagle-flying legions of Pompey and Marc Antony, Vespasian and Titus. Here, in these same Galilean hills, now a pleasant checkerboard of green and brown kibbutz lands, along the Via Maris, the great ancient highway from the Nile to the Euphrates, Deborah, the lady general, had vanquished the chariots of the Canaanites. Here, King Saul had met disaster at the hands of the Philistines, and Josiah was slain by the Egyptians, and Gideon's trumpet-blowing commandos blew a *nerve-krieg* that wiped out the Midianites. In the gentle hills overlooking Tiberias, known to history as the Horns of Hittin, the last of the great Crusades was smashed by the

Battle haze shrouds the Syrian countryside during the fight in the north.

Turks. And it was the sloping pastures of Megiddo, where Israeli paratroopers were now climbing into helicopters for the final assult on the fortified Syrian heights, that the New Testament Book of Revelation, in one of its most cryptic passages, had chosen for the last great battle of the world: the battle of Armageddon, which is in Hebrew *Har Megiddon,* hill of Megiddo.

Long after dark, the tank column continued to clatter across the narrow steel bridge over the Jordan and climbed up the bare, brown hills to Syria, and the air was a constant whir of helicopters. The jets came streaking in across the lake, pouring out cascades of napalm on Syria's "little Maginot Line," its ridgeline of concrete artillery emplacements and tank revetments. The night sky was everywhere alight with burning Syrian tanks and trucks, exploding shells, the white, hot puff of phosphorous bombs, like million-candlepower sparklers. A sliver of moon bathed the snowy tip of Mount Hermon in the soft sheen of old Arab silver, but the hills in between illuminated the sky in a false sunset glow of wheat

Victors of the Syrian campaign return from the front.

fields on fire, tanks and half-tracks in flames, the sudden secondary explosion of an ammunition truck or an oil tanker.

Gershon Fine, the gentle Hebrew scholar, stood at the barbed-wire gates of Kibbutz Ein Gev watching the destruction of the Syrian army, looking up with curiosity and wonder at the same heights which he and his comrades had looked at with fear and horror for nearly two decades.

"How the mighty are fallen, and the weapons of war perished," he said to his friend Benjamin Ben-Yosef, unabashedly borrowing his text from young David's lament for King Saul, who met his fate not so many miles away.

■ At dawn on this last day of war, at the other extreme of the fighting, Corporal Kamal Mahrouss saw a rose-colored blur. He knew immediately what it was: the red brick blockhouse at the Ismailia bridge. It meant that Kamal was in sight of the Suez Canal, in sight of home.

In four days he and the other escaping Egyptian soldiers had crossed the wretched wasteland of the Sinai, a 150-mile journey of agony and fear. He had done it partly by truck but mostly on foot through the powdery, ankle-deep sand that resisted every step. He had fought the unyielding heat, the searing thirst, the swarms of desert flies that had to be brushed constantly from his reddened eyes and cracked lips. He had known the desperate anxiety of the hunted, the torture of wondering whether the enemy lurked behind the next dune, or the next.

All this Kamal Mahrouss had endured and now it all was worth it because he was in sight of home. But he was not there yet.

Kamal drew nearer and the big square blockhouse took shape in the morning sun. Nearer still, and he saw the soldiers. And by their actions Kamal could tell that they saw him, too, him and his ragged Egyptian band of weary, wayworn desert wanderers. There was no use running. Kamal buried his gun and his compass in the sand and walked toward the enemy. Now, suddenly, his four-day ordeal seemed such a waste, such an injustice.

"Hello, Egyptians."

Kamal Mahrouss felt the sting of the smug, pseudo-friendly greeting. He made no reply.

Several Israeli soldiers approached and searched the captives. They took their cigaret lighters, identity cards, wedding rings, wristwatches.

"You're an Upper Egyptian, yes?" an Israeli officer asked Kamal. A good guess. Kamal's home was in the Nile Delta, the

151

Two Israelis at the Suez help an Egyptian homeward.

village of Menoufiya. But Kamal kept his silence.

"You seem to be as hardheaded as Mr. Nasser," said the officer. "You came to Sinai to kill us. Now we could kill you—but we won't." Then the officer turned to the entire group. "Which of you are officers and which are enlisted men?" he asked.

"We are all enlisted men," answered Kamal. It was not true. One of the men in the group was an officer, one of the six Kamal had found dying of thirst along the way and had revived. The Israeli officer continued:

"Do any of you know where Shepheard's Hotel is? Or Groppi's Place?"

Kamal knew. He had gone to school in Cairo and was familiar with both places, the hotel and the coffee shop, but he held his tongue.

"Cairo is a lovely place," said the officer, still trying to draw them out. Kamal said nothing.

At length the officer gave up—deciding, apparently, that the bedraggled group had no useful information to offer. He did not take them prisoner. He let them go.

The swing bridge across the Canal was out of operation. It was in the open position, parallel to the bank so ships could pass. Its pivoting mechanism was destroyed. The Egyptians had bombed it themselves the previous day to stall any Israeli advance across the Canal. Two hours later the Israelis wrecked it further, to stall the Egyptian retreat.

Kamal crossed the Canal in a small ferryboat. On the other side, he turned around and looked across the ribbon of water.

"We'll be back," he muttered. "Soon."

Frightened child clutches her toy amid the rubble of an air strike.

EPILOGUE

■ . . . and on the seventh day there was peace.

For six days the children of Abraham had had the blood of one another. Now it was time to place their fallen brethren beneath the earth. Now it was time to ponder the blackened stubble in the fields of milk and honey, time to shepherd the 100,000 refugees of a new exodus, time to ask if any amongst them—Jew or Arab—had found the justice they sought.

The Jew might say so. He had his sacred Wall again. His ships could pass in peace down the Gulf of Aqaba to the sea. But where was justice for the Arab who had seen his people scattered yet again?

The Jew had fought for survival against the *jihad*. He now held the land more securely. But wars do not take possession of the faith of a man. Napalm cannot burn out conviction and this the Arabs believed: they had been wronged and this they would right. Unhappily, this, too, the Jews believed—on the first day, when the war had begun, and on the seventh, when it was done.

The map had changed. Belief had not. "The war is over," said Moshe Dayan. "Now the trouble begins." He prophesied well.

The tiny David who had cowed his bullying tormentor now sought a Solomon to confirm the justice of his swift strike and bring him peace. But in New York, where the nations sit, he did not find it.

The French, the ally of Israel against Egypt in 1956, chided the Jews for starting the war. The United States, godfather of Israel at its birth, said the Jews must withdraw from the Arab land they had occupied.

154

Kosygin: the denouncer

Britain, which had made the first promise to the Jews, cautioned them against annexing the Old City. Russia called on the UN to denounce Israel as an aggressor and compel her to withdraw unconditionally back into her former borders. In the world Israel found few friends to speak up for her and, ironically, chief of them was West Germany where trade unions raised $750,000 to help Israel. Even India, whose stress in the Vale of Kashimir was not dissimilar to Israel's, somehow found it possible to righteously denounce Israel as a war maker.

Abba Eban, Israel's foreign minister, came to the UN and put the matter with logic and eloquence.

"The General Assembly witnessed an unusual spectacle this morning," he said. "The government of the United Arab Republic, which announced its intention to exterminate Israel, which concentrated 90,000 troops and 900 tanks for that purpose, which issued operation orders in mid-May to its commanders in the field for bombardment of Israel's airfields, which imposed a total blockade of Israel's entire southern coast, which called on other governments to join in a war of extermination against Israel, which expressed in mid-May and early June that Israel's end was near—this government comes to this tribune to present itself as a victim of aggression."

Surely no Solomon could deny the force of that argument. But the judges also heard from Jordan's King Hussein, he, too, a victim of the fated fratricide of the Middle East.

"We know, of course, that world sympathy for the Jews created Israel in the first place. But world sympathy for a tragic past does not permit condoning aggressive acts on the part of those who once were victims of aggression. Israel has stated that what its people want is peace and security, which has always been the cry of the successful aggressor. Peace by submission of the victim and security for what he has stolen. What Jordan and the Arabs want, on the other hand, is peace with justice.

"Today's war is not a new war but part of the old war which will go on for scores of years if the moral and physical wrong done to the Arabs is not righted."

The Arabs had reason to be aggrieved. Nasser had lost much of the $2 billion in arms Russia had sent him. The Suez Canal, which he counted on to produce $370 million of badly needed foreign exchange in 1967, was blocked by sunken ships. The country was almost broke and its wheat crop in peril. Jordan had lost the Old City and the tourist revenue of the pilgrims who came to it.

Maybe there was justice in this. But the Arabs did not see it.

Several days after the cease-fire, Cairo's airport was closed as big Antinov transports shuttled arms into Egypt from Russia. It was said Russia had supplied 50 to 80 MIGs.

On a hill in Syria an Israeli officer turned to a newsman. "We still can't quite believe that the war should be over so quickly." A shell from a Syrian cannon exploded nearby. The officer smiled. "See what I mean?"

The war had killed 20,000 Jordanians and perhaps as many Egyptians. Nasser had lost 700 tanks in the Sinai. Israel said it had lost 679 soldiers killed. But the balm their blood had bought only came in the form of the big Antinov transports with their killing cargoes.

And the cease-fire did not end all the bloodshed. There were intermittent outbreaks of fighting in subsequent days.

The Premier of the nation that was rearming the Arab, Alexei Kosygin, came to the United States. He called Israel the aggressor. He met with President Johnson and the world hoped the two poles of the world's might could somehow reach accord. They met in the small New Jersey college town of Glassboro. Kosygin said the talks had been "useful." Johnson said the world had become "a little less dangerous." But if they talked peace, they did not bring it.

It was Russia which called for an emergency meeting of the UN General Assembly. The delegates reached no conclusion, only voting down a Russian proposal to condemn Israel for aggression and require her to give up the taken land.

Hussein called for an Arab summit conference. He spoke moderation. He had been to Washington to see Johnson and said agreement might be reached with Israel over Jerusalem. "I'm not saying it's possible, and I'm not saying it's impossible."

Yet no one could speak for the Arabs. Nasser had called for an oil embargo of the Western powers. But within hours after the war ended, pumps in Saudi Arabia were at work again, loading American tankers.

One Arab nation would do business with the West while in another Nasser called on housewives to surrender their wedding rings. Money was needed for arms. An Egyptian woman wrote:

"There is only one dominant feeling that reigns in us: we have lost one round, but it is only one. We are determined on having it out with Israel. We will bury her in the sea."

Had no one learned anything from it all?

At the lakeside fish restaurant in Kibbutz Ein Gev, Gershon Fine looked up at the Syrian hills where the Israeli army was now encamped. He could not believe there would be no more shells.

"If ever there was a righteous war, and I am a man of peace, this was it," he said to his friend, Benjamin Ben-Yosef. "But now we must think no more of war. I believe that some day, maybe from now on, we will live in peace with our Arab neighbors. They are Semites, like us, and it is to our natural benefit to live in peace."

Eban: the defender

Not too far away, in Amman, Major Jamil, the tough professional of the Arab Legion, lay in his bed in a hospital. Several days after the cease-fire he had prevailed on two priests to drive him to the Allenby Bridge. He found a taxi on the other side to take him to Amman.

There, other officers told him of an Arab Legion tank named for the King—*Hussein Ibn Talal*—and how it had been damaged by the Israelis and how fiercely the Legionnaires had fought to bring it back to Jordan.

That was good. That was the way he knew the Legion would fight. Major Jamil vowed that, with Allah's will, he would return to fight again someday. And win.

Back in Egypt after his tortured trek

Hussein: the defeated

157

across the Sinai, Corporal Kamal Mahrouss also vowed. He firmly believed President Nasser's charge of American intervention. One day he would fight them, he said, in Viet Nam if necessary, to take his vengeance. America and Israel would pay for what they had done, he said.

On his cot in a prison camp south of Haifa, Colonel Mohamed Galal had other worries. His eyes moist, he puffed reflectively on a cigarette. He had learned from another prisoner that his old military academy chum who had stopped off at his artillery brigade back at Wadi el Arish had been killed.

"Perhaps," said Galal, "it is better to be killed in the field than to be a prisoner of war. Here you can't move. There's nothing to do . . . and I don't know what happened to my men . . ."

Sitting up in his hospital bed at the Hadassah Medical Center, Captain Matan Goor talked to some of his students who had hitchhiked all the way from Pardess Hana where he taught biology.

"We must keep the Syrian heights," he told them. "We must see to it that our people can visit the places in the Holy City that were promised to them 19 years ago but have been denied them ever since.

"I am not a religious man, but we must guarantee that, even if it means retaining old Jerusalem. The Sinai we don't need and don't want. We don't need territory. What we need most is to find a way for all of us, Arabs and Jews, to live in peace."

Rashid Areikat stood at the gates of Aqabat Jaber, one of the four refugee camps he administered for UNRWA, watching the people stream down the road and across the Jordan.

"These people waited 20 years for salvation. Now they are giving up. If there is to be peace, there must be justice. Arabs can live side by side with Jews. We have before. We can again. But there must be justice. The refugee problem can't be swept under the diplomatic rug for another 20 years without it all breaking out all over again."

Justice. Yes, justice. But who was there to give it? Who was there to say what it should be?

". . . but there must be justice."

STAFF FOR THIS BOOK

Editor: Saul Pett

Narrative by: Hugh Mulligan, John Barbour, Jules Loh, Sid Moody, William L. Ryan

Photo and Art Editors: Hal Buell, Max Desfer, Ed Fleming

Designer: Barbara H. White

Reporters (listed by home bureaus)
  Amman: Spiro Elissa
  Beirut: Roy Essoyan, Elias Antar, David Lancashire
  Cairo: Garven Hudgins, Aly Mahmoud, Hanns Neuerbourg, Ahmed Shawki
  Damascus: Farouk Nassar
  Geneva: Michael Goldsmith
  Jerusalem: Eric Gottgetreu
  London: Lawrence Malkin, Thomas A. Reedy
  Nairobi: Dennis Neeld
  Nicosia: Alex Efty
  Oslo: George Boultwood
  Rome: David Mazzarella
  Tel Aviv: Hal McClure, Paul Kohn, Andrew Meisels
  Vienna: Hans Benedict

Photographers
  Amman: Hagop Touranian
  Beirut: Harry Koundakjian
  Cairo: Ahmed el Tayeb
  Frankfort: Bernhard Frye, Kurt Strumpf
  Jerusalem (Jordan): Ali Zaroor
  London: Brian Calvert, Frank Tewkesbury, Eddie Worth
  Malta: Arrigo Azzopardi
  Milan: Raoul Fornezza
  Nicosia: Themis Joanidis
  Paris: Jacques Marqueton, Michael Nash, Spartaco Bodini, Michel Lipchitz
  Tel Aviv and Jerusalem: Hans Pinn, Mrs. Suzy Pinn, Jack Goren, Mordecai Dekel, Isaac Berez, Oscar Tauber

Artists: George Braunsdorf, Jack Elcik